Conquering the SAT and ACT Exams

with Julia Ross

Julia Ross

Edited by Rachel Knitzer

We want to hear from you. Please send your comments about this book to us in care of the address below. Thank you.

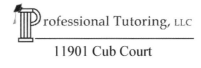

11901 Cub Court

Fairfax Station, VA 22039

ISBN: 1974502465

ISBN-13: 978-1974502462

For more information on the services offered by Professional Tutoring, LLC, visit **www.JuliaRossPT.com**

Contents

Chapter 1

Introduction to College Admissions

In this chapter:

- What Is the SAT Exam?

- SAT Redesigned Exam Overview

- What is the ACT Exam?

- ACT Exam Overview

- Rules for Taking the Exams

- Strategies for the Exams

- Guidelines for Studying for Your SAT/ACT Score

- SAT vs. ACT Scoring Comparison

- Admissions Probability Organizer

- Rubric for Essay on SAT/ACT Score Goals

- SAT/ACT Exam Scores Charts: Diagnostic, Practice, Goal

- Registering for Your Tests: Administration Dates & Registration Guidelines

- Test Day Advice

What Is the SAT Exam?

SAT Redesigned Exam

- Knowledge and reasoning based exam
- 3-hour exam with 4 Multiple Choice Sections, total of 154 questions
- Optional 50-min Essay
- 2 sub-scores, each worth up to 800 points:

  <u>Evidence-Based Reading & Writing</u>   <u>Mathematics</u>
- Most colleges do not require essay
- Score is total of the 2 sub-scores; Maximum score is 1600
- $46 registration fee, $60 with essay
- Saturday exam days

SAT Subject Exams

- Content-based exams that allow student to demonstrate achievement
- One hour per exam with up to 3 tests per registration
- 20 Exams offered in 5 subject areas:

  <u>English</u>   <u>History</u>   <u>Math</u>   <u>Science</u>   <u>Foreign Languages</u>
- Exams are in a multiple-choice format
- $26 registration fee plus $21 per test
- Subject tests are not available in March
- Subject Exams and Redesigned Exam cannot be taken on the same day
- Recommended for admission into elite/competitive universities

When Should I take the SAT Exam?

- Exams are offered 7 times throughout the year:

  August, October, November, December, March, May, June
- <u>May & June</u> SAT exams for <u>junior year</u> recommended
- <u>November & December</u> SAT exams for <u>senior year</u> recommended

www.CollegeBoard.com

Redesigned SAT Exam Overview

The SAT tests critical reading, math, and writing. The following will give you a general overview of the test and some basic strategies that will help you gain confidence in attaining a better score.

SAT Format

The SAT is 3 hours long with a few 10-minute breaks in between sections. The exam is mostly made up of multiple choice questions and is divided into the following sections:

	Section	Length	Content	Type	# of Questions
1.	Reading Test	65 Minutes	Reading Comprehension, vocabulary in context	Multiple Choice	52
2.	Writing & Language	35 Minutes	Grammar, vocabulary in context, and editing skills	Multiple Choice	44
3.	Math w/o calculator	25 Minutes	HS geometry and algebra, numbers and operations, statistics, probability and data analysis	Multiple Choice and Grid-ins	20
4.	Math w/ calculator	55 Minutes	Same as above	Multiple Choice and Grid-ins	38
5.	Essay (optional)	50 Minutes	Analyze how author builds an argument	Essay	1

Scoring

1. You gain one point for each correct answer on the SAT.

2. You don't lose any points for incorrect answers or questions left blank.

3. Also, you don't lose any points for wrong answers in the math grid-in section.

4. Each section (Reading/Writing and Math) is worth 800 points, and the total maximum score for the entire SAT exam is 1600 points. The optional Essay section is scored out of a possible 24 points.

What Is the ACT Exam?

ACT Exam

- Achievement test that is knowledge and curriculum-based
- Measures high school achievement
- 2-hour 55-minute exam with 215 multiple choice questions
- Made up of 4 sections each worth up to 36 points:

  <u>English</u>   <u>Mathematics</u>   <u>Reading</u>   <u>Science</u>

- Optional 40-minute Writing Section available
- Composite score is the average of the 4 sections, Maximum composite score is 36
- Writing section scored from 2-12
- $42.50 registration fee or $58.50 fee with Writing Section
- Saturday exam days

ACT Subject Exams

- ACT does not offer subject tests

When Should I take the ACT Exam?

- ACT Exams are offered 7 times throughout the year:
  September, October, December, February, April, June, July
- <u>April & June</u> ACT exams for <u>junior year</u> recommended
- <u>October & December</u> ACT exams for <u>senior year</u> recommended

www.ACT.org

ACT Exam Overview

The ACT tests English, reading, math, and science. The following will give you a general overview of the test and some basic strategies that will help you gain confidence in attaining a better score.

ACT Format

The ACT is 2 hours and 55 minutes long with a 10-minute break in between the math and reading tests. If you choose to take the writing test, you will also get a 5-minute break after the science test. The exam is completely made up of multiple choice questions and is divided into the following sections:

	Section	Length	Content	Type	# of Questions
1.	English Test	45 Minutes	Grammar, vocabulary in context, and editing skills	Multiple Choice	75
2.	Math Test	60 Minutes	HS geometry and algebra, numbers and operations, statistics, probability and data analysis	Multiple Choice	60
3.	Reading Test	35 Minutes	Reading Comprehension	Multiple Choice	40
4.	Science Test	35 Minutes	General scientific knowledge, data analysis, experimental design	Multiple Choice	40
5.	Writing Test (optional)	40 Minutes	Analyze and compare different perspectives on an issue	Essay	1

ACT Scoring

1. You gain one point for each correct answer on the ACT. This raw score is then converted to a scale score from 1-36.

2. You don't lose any points for incorrect answers or questions left blank.

3. Also, you don't lose any points for wrong answers in the math grid-in section.

4. Each section (English, Math, Reading, and Science) is scored from 1-36 points, and the composite score for the entire ACT test is the average of those four scores. The optional Essay section is scored out of a possible 12 points.

Rules for taking the Exams

1) You cannot jump back and forth between timed sections.

2) You cannot return to earlier sections to change your answers.

3) You cannot spend any additional time in a section once your time is up.

4) You can move around within a section as much as you want.

5) You can look ahead within a section to see (or preview) what kinds of questions are coming.

Strategies for the Exams

1. Directions never change, you will have them all memorized by the end of this course. SO DON'T WASTE TIME READING THEM. However, you MUST closely read the document/perspectives above the essay question. The background given in this section will provide direction for your ENTIRE essay.

2. Make an educated guess rather than leaving a question blank. You don't lose any points for guessing in the new SAT or ACT.

3. Answer ALL grid-ins in the SAT-even if it's your telephone number. You have nothing to lose.

4. Check your answer sheet once in a while to make sure your answers and questions are lined up.

5. Circle the questions you decide to answer later so they're easy to find.

6. Wear a watch and keep track of the time—especially when reading long passages.

7. Read the question carefully before you look at the answer choices.

8. Try to make up your own answer (prediction) before you even look at the answer choices.

9. Find a couple of quick points if you are running out of time especially if you are working on reading comprehension.

Guidelines for Studying for Your SAT and ACT Exams

Weekly Review:

1. Attend class, pay attention. Do not sit near a friend or other distraction. Make sure that you sit where you can see the whiteboard well. I see lots of squinting.

2. Make sure to ask questions in class. It is very important that you direct questions to your instructors. They cannot differentiate between chatting and "working" with another student.

3. Complete your homework carefully. Check all the answers in the back of the workbook, vocabulary book and the test book.

4. Form a study group of two to three students. <u>Commit and meet weekly!</u> See below for study group ideas.

Reading and Writing Review:

1. Review vocabulary (current and old lists) 4-5 times per week for 15-20 minutes per session. This is crucial to your success on both the Reading and Writing sections. Prepare for vocabulary quizzes.

2. Parents, please review the lists and try to use these words in your daily household conversations. One pitfall is that students use the literal meaning (denotation) and miss the connotation. Students often need help remembering the pronunciation; this helps the kids to remember the words and recognize them in reading and in conversation.

3. Read for pleasure!! Some good books include: *The Hot Zone*, the *Harry Potter* series, *Gone with the Wind*, *Jane Eyre*, etc.

4. Re-read the initial assignments (in the College Board book and ACT book) in the syllabus.

5. Review the Reading Overview in Chapter Two.

6. Review the Writing Overview and worksheets in Chapter Three.

Math Review:

Go over the practice math exercises included in this book, especially any of the lessons that you found difficult in class. Re-do problems until you understand! Prepare for math quizzes.

<u>Testing Review:</u>

Students may review tests numbered 5-8 in the College Board test book. It is a really good idea to work on practice problems.

<u>Form a Study Group:</u>

It is important to set up study groups. While our kids should be mature enough to do this on their own, this is usually not the case. The set-up and initial sessions require consistent parental involvement. My recommendations for study groups are:

1. Students may review ONLY tests numbered 5-8 in the College Board test book. It is a really good idea to work on practice problems.

2. Choose a group of 2-3 students for a study group (parents and students should do this collaboratively).

3. Students should make contact with their chosen study group. If they do not do so within a specified time period as agreed at home, parents should contact parents.

4. Study groups should plan on 2-hour sessions once or twice per week.

5. In the study group, students should do the following:

    - Homework

    - Vocabulary review (current and old words)

    - Practice SAT/ACT questions

6. Parents should help facilitate the meeting by remaining in the study room for the entire two-hour period for at least the first 4-6 sessions. Parents can help by making vocabulary flashcards, quizzing on the vocabulary words, working out any reading/math/writing problems.

7. Set up a specific study group time that does NOT vary EVER. Even if only one student can make the study group, go ahead and have it. Once changes begin, it is really hard to get back on track.

8. Feeding the kids does work wonders too!

How many questions do I have to answer correctly to achieve my goal scores?

SAT Exam

96 Reading/Writing Questions   58 Math Problems   154 Total questions

SAT Exam		96	58	154		
Score	ACT	Rdg/Writ.	Math	Total	Percentage	Grade
1000	19	51	26	77	50%	F
1100	22	55	32	87	56%	F
1200	25	65	38	103	67%	D
1300	27	74	44	118	77%	C
1400	30	82	50	132	86%	B
1500	33	89	54	143	93%	A-
1600	36	95	58	153	99%	A

ACT Exam

75 English Questions   60 Math Questions   40 Reading Questions

40 Science Questions   215 Total Questions on the ACT Exam

ACT Exam		75	60	40	40	215		
Score	SAT	English	Math	Reading	Science	Total	Percentage	Grade
19	1000	42.5	26.5	22.5	16.50	108.0	50%	F
22	1100	51.0	31.5	27.5	23.00	133.0	62%	F
25	1200	59.0	37.5	31.0	28.50	156.0	73%	C
27	1300	63.5	42.0	33.0	31.00	169.5	79%	C+
30	1400	68.0	47.5	38.0	34.00	187.5	87%	B
33	1500	71.0	52.5	40.0	37.00	200.5	93%	A-
36	1600	75.0	59.0	36.0	39.50	209.5	97%	A

Please note: each official SAT/ACT test varies slightly in how the raw score (how many questions you got right) is converted to a scaled score. The numbers in these charts should be used as guidelines, not guarantees.

SAT vs. ACT Scoring Comparison

New SAT Total (400-1600)	ACT Composite Score	New SAT Total (400-1600)	ACT Composite Score	New SAT Total (400-1600)	ACT Composite Score
1600	36	1250	26	900	17
1590	35	1240	26	890	16
1580	35	1230	25	880	16
1570	35	1220	25	870	16
1560	35	1210	25	860	16
1550	34	1200	25	850	15
1540	34	1190	24	840	15
1530	34	1180	24	830	15
1520	34	1170	24	820	15
1510	33	1160	23	810	15
1500	33	1150	23	800	14
1490	33	1140	23	790	14
1480	32	1130	23	780	14
1470	32	1120	22	770	14
1460	32	1110	22	760	14
1450	32	1100	22	750	13
1440	31	1090	21	740	13
1430	31	1080	21	730	13
1420	31	1070	21	720	13
1410	30	1060	21	710	12
1400	30	1050	20	700	12
1390	30	1040	20	690	12
1380	29	1030	20	680	12
1370	29	1020	20	670	12
1360	29	1010	19	660	12
1350	29	1000	19	650	12
1340	28	990	19	640	12
1330	28	980	19	630	11
1320	28	970	18	620	11
1310	27	960	18	610	11
1300	27	950	18	600	11
1290	27	940	18	590	11
1280	27	930	17	580	11
1270	26	920	17	570	11
1260	26	910	17	560	11

Please note: This data is endorsed by the College Board only. The ACT organization does not guarantee its accuracy.

Admissions Probability Organizer

Weighted Grade Point Average

Safety School	Safety School	Attainable School	Reach School	Reach School
- .3	- .2	Your GPA	+.2	+.3

SAT Scores

Safety School	Safety School	Attainable School	Reach School	Reach School
- 150 pts.	- 100 pts.	Reading + Math	+ 100 pts.	+ 150 pts.

ACT Scores

Safety School	Safety School	Attainable School	Reach School	Reach School
- 4pts.	- 3 pts.	Your ACT	+ 3 pts.	+ 4 pts.

Professional Tutoring, LLC - Virginia Public Universities Admissions Data
(Fairfax County Public School Students - Class of 2016 - Listed by Average Accepted SAT Score) *

College	SAT Avg.	SAT Min.	ACT Avg.	ACT Min.	GPA Avg. Weighted	GPA Min. Weighted	Applied	Accepted	Yield
College of William and Mary	1419	900	31	20	4.23	3.24	1607	47%	30%
University of Virginia	1416	960	31	20	4.32	3.25	2554	41%	58%
Virginia Tech	1305	780	29	14	4.07	2.01	3351	65%	43%
James Madison University	1219	690	27	15	3.84	2.45	2940	66%	30%
George Mason University	1203	680	26	14	3.77	1.83	3484	73%	35%
Christopher Newport U.	1199	710	26	14	3.72	2.52	1219	64%	21%
Virginia Military Institute	1178	850	26	19	3.54	2.55	88	59%	48%
Virginia Commonwealth U.	1173	740	25	13	3.62	2.03	2720	79%	30%
U. of Mary Washington	1131	710	24	13	3.57	2.03	1108	78%	20%
Longwood University	1059	690	23	13	3.29	2.27	525	75%	16%
Old Dominion University	1049	670	22	12	3.22	1.41	1129	80%	24%
Radford University	1023	590	22	12	3.07	1.67	775	82%	25%
UVA Wise	1000	650	21	15	3.07	2.08	45	80%	36%
Virginia State University	880	560	17	12	2.79	2.08	96	57%	40%
Norfolk State University	874	670	17	12	2.88	1.93	74	55%	34%

*Data compiled by Professional Tutoring, LLC.

Professional Tutoring, LLC - Most Popular Out-of-State and Private Colleges
(Fairfax County Public School Students - Class of 2016 - Listed Alphabetically) *

Name of Institution	SAT Av. Accepted	SAT Min. Accepted	ACT Av. Accepted	ACT Min. Accepted	GPA Av. Accepted	GPA Min. Accepted	Applied	Accepted	Yield
Appalachian State University (NC)	1206	1010	26	20	3.71	3.13	44	73%	25%
Auburn University (AL)	1202	940	27	19	3.69	2.84	108	86%	19%
Boston College (MA)	1403	1020	31	22	4.23	3.57	132	33%	7%
Boston University (MA)	1351	760	30	22	4.09	2.87	284	40%	10%
Carnegie Mellon University (PA)	1488	990	33	24	4.30	3.28	337	24%	43%
The Citadel (SC)	1077	840	23	15	3.31	2.23	26	96%	40%
Clemson University (SC)	1281	690	29	15	3.98	2.44	304	62%	17%
College of Charleston (SC)	1155	890	25	18	3.52	2.40	88	90%	19%
Duke University (NC)	1496	1090	33	28	4.40	3.46	384	11%	57%
Duquesne University (PA)	1143	960	27	19	3.60	2.41	33	85%	32%
East Carolina University (NC)	1066	800	23	17	3.33	2.48	173	73%	29%
Elon University (NC)	1241	1030	29	20	3.89	2.57	130	57%	20%
Emory University (GA)	1468	1230	32	27	4.28	3.68	116	26%	17%
Florida State University (FL)	1192	920	26	19	3.70	2.43	89	65%	26%
Georgetown University (DC)	1439	980	32	22	4.24	2.38	325	15%	51%
Georgia Tech (GA)	1456	1030	33	25	4.35	3.27	347	33%	16%
Hampden-Sydney College (VA)	1229	960	27	20	3.56	2.77	42	79%	15%
Ivy League Average	1491	1234	33	29	4.32	3.75	1655	10%	48%
Johns Hopkins University (MD)	1447	1080	32	23	4.31	3.86	328	11%	43%
Lafayette College (PA)	1336	1200	29	23	4.09	3.11	46	37%	35%

*Data compiled by Professional Tutoring, LLC.

Name of Institution	SAT Av. Accepted	SAT Min. Accepted	ACT Av. Accepted	ACT Min. Accepted	GPA Av. Accepted	GPA Min. Accepted	Applied	Accepted	Yield
Lehigh University (PA)	1370	1100	30	25	4.10	3.52	80	39%	26%
Louisiana State University (LA)	1122	830	25	12	3.45	1.67	63	84%	13%
Lynchburg College (VA)	1056	710	23	13	3.23	1.89	149	85%	18%
Marymount University (VA)	1002	600	21	14	3.32	2.03	298	79%	31%
Mass. Inst. Technology - MIT (MA)	1524	1290	34	33	4.46	4.14	221	10%	86%
Miami University, Oxford (OH)	1285	970	29	21	3.83	2.95	136	73%	20%
Michigan State University (MI)	1203	880	27	18	3.63	2.87	59	75%	18%
New York University (NY)	1391	840	31	19	4.14	2.90	356	41%	20%
North Carolina State University (NC)	1259	730	28	19	3.95	2.51	202	49%	6%
The Ohio State University (OH)	1316	880	30	14	4.01	2.88	201	63%	17%
Penn. State University (PA)	1236	760	27	17	3.77	2.40	708	87%	19%
Purdue University (IN)	1366	1010	31	23	4.02	2.97	261	66%	21%
Shenandoah University (VA)	1030	670	21	15	3.19	2.05	156	76%	31%
Rochester Institute of Technology (NY)	1309	970	29	19	3.77	2.19	92	92%	32%
Syracuse University (NY)	1275	970	28	18	3.80	2.88	154	58%	18%
Stanford University (CA)	1477	1240	34	31	4.46	4.28	331	5%	94%
Texas Christian University (TX)	1180	980	28	22	3.78	2.85	24	42%	20%
The George Washington University (DC)	1328	900	29	22	4.12	2.55	487	37%	23%
Tulane University (LA)	1346	1090	31	28	3.92	3.00	112	23%	8%
University of Alabama (AL)	1157	740	25	17	3.44	1.96	197	91%	23%
University of California Berkeley (CA)	1508	1200	33	25	4.40	4.00	254	25%	27%

Name of Institution	SAT Av. Accepted	SAT Min. Accepted	ACT Av. Accepted	ACT Min. Accepted	GPA Av. Accepted	GPA Min. Accepted	Applied	Accepted	Yield
University of California, Los Angeles (CA)	1452	1030	32	22	4.31	2.43	194	29%	18%
University of Chicago (IL)	1521	1300	34	31	4.36	3.89	279	11%	68%
University of Colorado at Boulder (CO)	1232	830	28	14	3.72	2.30	143	70%	23%
University of Connecticut (CT)	1306	1010	30	18	3.87	3.03	43	72%	10%
University of Delaware (DE)	1236	970	28	22	3.86	2.79	155	75%	15%
University of Florida (FL)	1252	920	28	22	3.92	3.44	76	63%	40%
University of Maryland, College Park (MD)	1346	740	30	17	4.06	1.96	501	57%	14%
University of Miami (FL)	1351	1020	31	21	4.06	3.18	131	56%	19%
University of Michigan (MI)	1466	1150	33	24	4.33	3.46	417	26%	24%
University of Mississippi (MS)	1124	800	25	19	3.35	2.31	90	90%	27%
University of New Hampshire (NH)	1201	920	27	22	3.72	3.20	27	78%	10%
UNC Chapel Hill (NC)	1466	1010	33	26	4.32	3.28	402	19%	14%
University of Notre Dame (IN)	1481	1350	34	31	4.35	4.17	98	19%	37%
University of Pittsburgh (PA)	1324	900	30	17	3.90	2.53	347	90%	22%
University of Rhode Island (RI)	1198	890	25	13	3.47	2.54	20	60%	25%
University of Richmond (VA)	1305	860	29	22	4.10	3.14	195	33%	20%
University of South Carolina (SC)	1198	920	27	12	3.70	2.17	330	82%	22%
University of Tennessee (TN)	1155	850	24	17	3.52	2.49	98	91%	20%
University of Texas, Austin (TX)	1356	1020	31	21	4.13	3.44	148	24%	23%
University of Vermont (VT)	1284	940	28	22	3.85	3.05	70	74%	19%
University of Wisconsin (WI)	1330	900	30	19	4.07	3.46	87	57%	8%
U.S Service Academies Academy Avg	1299	1016	28	23	3.95	3.25	144	29%	74%

Rubric for Essay on SAT/ACT Score Goals

You will each prepare a five-paragraph essay for me detailing your college and SAT/ACT exam goals. Goal setting and visualization play a critical role in success. Take time to sit down with your parents and discuss your future. Use the following format. Impress me!! ☺

1st Paragraph: In this paragraph you will write about your family and background. Tell me where you grew up, how many members in your family, your interests.

2nd Paragraph: In this paragraph, you will write about your schooling and academic experience up to now (your junior/senior year). Begin with a sketch of your primary school years (1st – 6th grades) and then your middle and upper school years. Have you enjoyed school? What parts do you like best? Tell me about the classes that you found most interesting. What have you found most interesting/easiest/most difficult? Do you participate in extra-curricular activities?

3rd Paragraph: What do you plan to do after high school? Will you immediately enroll in a four-year college/university? Do you have a dream school? What majors are you considering? What do you want to do as an adult?

4th Paragraph: Please analyze the SAT and ACT exams that you took in the beginning of the course. Do you notice any patterns? Was one section easier for you than the others? Did you finish each section? Did you omit lots of questions, few or none? What did you do well? What did not go so well?

5th Paragraph: Now it is time to set your goals for the two sections of the SAT exam and the four sections of the ACT. As we discussed in class, you will base your goals on several criteria:
1. Your College Dreams;
2. Your GPA;
3. Your work ethic and time commitment to studying for this class; and
4. Discussion with your parents.

NAME: _____   Date: _____

SAT DIAGNOSTIC SCORE:

    Reading/Writing: _____ Math: _____ Essay: _____

    Total: _____

SAT GOAL SCORE:

    Reading/Writing: _____ Math: _____ Essay: _____

    Total: _____

ACT DIAGNOSTIC SCORE:

      English: _____   Math: _____   Reading: _____

      Science: _____   Essay: _____

      Total: _____

ACT GOAL SCORE:

      English: _____   Math: _____   Reading: _____

      Science: _____   Essay: _____

      Total: _____

Exam Scores: Diagnostic, Practice, Goal

SAT Goals and Scores Sheet

Name: _____ Class Session: _____ P.T. ID#: _____

Test	Date Taken	Critical Reading	Math	Essay	CR/Math Subtotal	Total	Change
Diagnostic CB # _____							
SAT Goal Score							
PSAT - 10th Grade							
PSAT - 11th Grade							
Practice Test CB # _____							
Practice Test CB # _____							
Practice Test CB # _____							
Practice Test CB # _____							
Best Scores							
SAT Exam #1							
SAT Exam #2							

ACT Goals and Scores Sheet

Name: _____ Class Session: _____ P.T. ID#: _____

Test	Date Taken	English	Math	Reading	Science	Writing	Comp. Score	Change
Diagnostic ACT # _____								
ACT Goal Score								
Practice Test ACT # _____								
Practice Test ACT # _____								
Practice Test ACT # _____								
Practice Test ACT # _____								
Best Scores								
ACT Test #1								
ACT Test #2								

Registering for Your Tests

Approximate SAT Administration Dates & Registration Deadlines

* Dates can change each year. The dates indicated here are cautious planning dates. Verify dates at CollegeBoard.com

Test Dates	Registration Deadline	Late Registration
August	July 25	August 15
October	September 1	September 15
November	October 1	October 15
December	November 1	November 15
March	February 1	February 15
May	April 1	April 15
June	May 1	May 15

Registration:

For Juniors: Register by **February 1**st for the May **and** the June exams. Register for your base school or another local school.

For Seniors: Register by **September 1**st for the November **and** the December exams. Register for your base school or another local school.

Website: CollegeBoard.org

SAT Registration Guidelines

SAT Redesigned Exam:

Juniors: The Professional Tutoring SAT/ACT Preparation nine-month and six-month courses prepare 10th and 11th graders for the SAT Redesigned Exam, which satisfies college/university admission test requirements. This is a three-hour test with an optional 50-minute writing section. Excluding the writing section, the test must be taken as a whole; students cannot take a subset of the test. As far as I know, there is no limit to the number of times that one may sit for the SAT. This SAT/ACT Preparation Course prepares students to take the SAT exam two times (May and June). In general, students achieve their highest score after finishing the class.

Seniors: This class prepares rising 12th graders for the SAT Redesigned Exam, which satisfies college/university admission test requirements. This is a three-hour test with an optional 50-minute writing section. Excluding the writing section, the test must be taken as a whole; students cannot take a subset of the test. As far as I know, there is no limit to the number of times that one may sit for the SAT. This SAT Preparation Course prepares students to take the exam two times during their senior year (November and December). In general, students achieve their highest score after finishing the class.

SAT Subject Tests:

SAT Subject Exams (formerly known as the SAT II Exams) include 20 subject-specific tests which measure a student's knowledge in five subject areas: English, history, languages, mathematics and science. In general, elite colleges require SAT Subject Tests for admission. MOST colleges do NOT require/recommend SAT Subject Exams. Most students try to take the SAT Subject Tests as close to completing an AP or an IB class as possible. As the SAT Subject Tests are one hour long; students may register to take up to three exams at one sitting. Most students find that they can only handle two exams on a single test date. **Do NOT** underestimate these exams; they are hard, and most students are not prepared after taking the first level of a course, e.g. freshman biology! Professional Tutoring, LLC, offers tutoring for many of the SAT Subject Tests.

Exam Dates:

SAT Redesigned and SAT Subject exams are offered on the same dates throughout the school year. Students may take either the SAT Redesigned Exam <u>or</u> up to three SAT Subject Tests at one sitting. Not all Subject Tests are available on every date and no Subject Tests are given in March.

Registration:

Students may register for both the SAT Redesigned and SAT Subject exams on-line at <u>www.collegeboard.org</u>. Students should register for **both** the May and June SAT Redesigned exams. It is best to register for the exams as early as possible to ensure a space **at your base school exam center**. Make sure to write down your College Board user name and password for future reference; you will need these repeatedly in the upcoming months!

ID Requirements: Students are required to show a photo ID to take the exam. The photo ID must have a clear photograph that matches the test-taker, and must be one that is government issued (i.e. driver's license, passport, or military ID) <u>or</u> ID from the school you currently attend <u>or</u> the notarized *College Board Student ID Form* (available from school counselor and prepared by the school). Acceptable ID must be original, valid, current and have your full name exactly as it appears on the Admission Ticket.

Photo Submission: As of the March 2013 SAT Exams, the College Board is requiring a digital submission of an identifying photograph at registration. This photograph will become part of the student's test registration and Admission Ticket and will be compared to the student's approved photo ID at the test site.

<u>Photo requirements:</u>
- Submit during online registration
- Photograph, preferably digital and not copy
- Clear and in focus with good lighting, full face view, only head and shoulders
- Digital specs: Minimum of 325 X 390 pixels, formatted in .jpg or .gif or .png.
- Religious head-coverings must match photo ID and in-person at test site

Test Day Entrance: In-person appearance MUST match photo well. Students must have both the photo admission ticket <u>and</u> an acceptable form of photo ID for entry to the test center and upon entry of the test room and for the collection of answer sheets.

Scores: Students may view their scores approximately two weeks after completing the exam (www.collegeboard.org – user name and password required). We recommend that Professional Tutoring SAT Preparation students take the SAT Redesigned Exam only two times during the course (May and June for juniors, November and December for seniors). Most students will achieve their highest scores in this short period. If the May score is excellent (surpasses the student's goal), some students will decide to forgo the June SAT Redesigned Exam and instead register late for one to three SAT Subject Tests in June.

<u>Accommodations:</u>	Students who have a current Individualized Education Plan or a 504 Plan or other in-school accommodations may be eligible for testing accommodations, such as additional testing time, bubbling support (circling answers in test booklet instead of bubbling) or a reader. If you are eligible for accommodations and have not yet begun to work with the College Board to set them up, see me!
<u>Certifications</u>:	Test proctors will be able to compare the picture on the Admission Ticket to both the photo ID the student presents as well as to the student's face. Test takers will also be required to sign a certification statement on the SAT answer sheet regarding accuracy of all submissions, complicity to testing security and acknowledgment of law enforcement issues for engaging in impersonation.
<u>Caveats:</u>	Students are responsible for understanding and following the SAT identification requirements and policies. Any questions should be addressed to Customer Service at the College Board (call 866-756-7346) well in advance of test day. It is your responsibility to ensure that your ID documents are up-to-date and available on the day of the test. Questionable ID is subject to College Board review and approval before, during or after the test administration.

Approximate ACT Administration Dates & Registration Deadlines

* Dates can change each year. The dates indicated here are cautious planning dates. Verify dates at ACT.org.

Test Dates	Registration Deadline	Late Registration
September	August 1	August 15
October	September 15	October 1
December	November 1	November 15
February	January 15	February 1
April	March 1	March 15
June	May 1	May 15
July	June 15	July 1

Registration:

For Juniors: Register by **February 1st** for the April **and** the June exams. Register for your base school or another local school.

For Seniors: Register by **September 1st** for the October **and** the December exams. Register for your base school or another local school.

Website: ACT.org

ACT Registration Guidelines

The ACT Test:

Juniors: The Professional Tutoring SAT/ACT Preparation nine-month and six-month courses prepare 10th and 11th graders for the ACT Test, which satisfies college/university admission test requirements. This is a 2-hour and 55-minute test with an optional 40-minute writing section. Excluding the writing section, the test must be taken as a whole; students cannot take a subset of the test. Students are permitted to take the ACT up to twelve times. This SAT/ACT Preparation Course prepares students to take the ACT exam two times (April and June). In general, students achieve their highest score after finishing the class.

Seniors: This class prepares rising 12th graders for the ACT Test, which satisfies college/university admission test requirements. This is a 2-hour 55-minute test with an optional 40-minute writing section. Excluding the writing section, the test must be taken as a whole; students cannot take a subset of the test. Students are permitted to take the ACT up to twelve times. This SAT/ACT Preparation Course prepares students to take each exam two times during their senior year (November and December). In general, students achieve their highest score after finishing the class.

Exam Dates:

The ACT is now offered seven times during the year. No exams are offered in August, November, January, March or May.

Registration:

Students may register for both the ACT Test on-line at www.act.org. Students should register for **both** the April and June ACT tests. It is best to register for the exams as early as possible to ensure a space **at your base school exam center**. Make sure to write down your ACT user name and password for future reference; you will need these repeatedly in the upcoming months!

ID Requirements:

Students are required to show a photo ID to take the exam. The photo ID must have a clear photograph that matches the test-taker, and must be one that is government issued (i.e. driver's license, passport, or military ID) <u>or</u> ID from the school you currently attend <u>or</u> the notarized *ACT Student Identification Form* (available from school counselor and prepared by the school). Acceptable ID must be original, valid, current, and have the student's name exactly as it appears on the ACT admissions ticket.

Photo Submission:

The ACT is now requiring a digital submission of an identifying photograph at registration. This photograph will become part of the student's test registration and admissions ticket and will be compared to the student's approved photo ID at the test site.

<u>Photo requirements</u>:
- Preferably digital and not copy
- Clear and in focus with good lighting, full face view, only head and shoulders, against a plain background
- Digital specs: Minimum of 640 X 480 pixels, formatted in .jpg, .jpeg, .png, or .bmp.
- Photo must be uploaded <u>at least</u> 8 days prior to test date
- Religious head-coverings must match photo and in-person at test site

<u>Test Day Entrance</u>:

In-person appearance MUST match photo well. Students must have both the photo admission ticket <u>and</u> an acceptable form of photo ID for entry to the test center and upon entry of the test room and for the collection of answer sheets.

<u>Scores</u>:

Students may view their scores within two weeks of completing the exam (www.act.org – user name and password required). We recommend that Professional Tutoring SAT/ACT Preparation students take the ACT Test only two times during the course (April and June). Most students will achieve their highest scores in this short period.

<u>Accommodations</u>:

Students who have a current Individualized Education Plan or a 504 Plan or who have testing accommodations at school may be eligible for testing accommodations, such as additional testing time, bubbling support or a reader. If you are eligible for accommodations and have not yet begun to work with the ACT to set them up, see me!

<u>Certifications</u>:

Test proctors will be able to compare the picture on the Admission Ticket to both the photo ID the student presents as well as to the student's face. Test takers will also be required to sign a certification statement on the ACT answer sheet regarding accuracy of all submissions, complicity to testing security and acknowledgment of law enforcement issues for engaging in impersonation.

<u>Caveats:</u>

Students are responsible for understanding and following the ACT identification requirements and policies. Any questions should be addressed to Customer Service at the ACT (call 319-337-1270) well in advance of test day. It is your responsibility to ensure that your ID documents are up-to-date and available on the day of the test. Questionable ID is subject to ACT review and approval before, during or after the test administration.

Test Day Advice: **

In 18 years of preparing students to take these exams, I have developed a list of test day tips:

- Register to take the SAT/ACT Exams at your local school, if offered. You will feel much more comfortable in your own environment.

- If you are not able to register for your base school, ask your parents to drive you to the test center. When a student gets lost or has trouble finding a parking spot, s/he will enter the test feeling stressed. This is not a good way to begin these critically important exams.

- Students should drive <u>with their parents or alone</u> to the test site. It is important to remain focused in the time leading to the exam.

- Make sure that everything is ready the night before the exam: driver's license, test admissions form, calculator, extra batteries (AAA), pencils, snack/lunch, change for the vending machines, and gas in the car.

- Rest the night before the exam – no cramming and no partying and no sleepovers! Prom/Homecoming often falls on the night before an SAT/ACT Exam, so plan accordingly.

- Eat a "normal" breakfast. Do not overdo or under do this meal.

- Pack a heavy snack/lunch to eat quickly during a break.

- You may bring water to the test center to have on your desk.

<u>Remember</u>:

Everyone should remember that the students will have completed an extensive SAT/ACT preparation course. You have done a great job studying and are so much more prepared than you were several months ago and so much readier than most everyone else!!

** Excerpted from *Getting into College with Julia Ross: Finding the Right Fit and Making It Happen* (2013)

Chapter 2

Critical Reading

In this chapter:

- SAT/ACT Reading Overview

- Reading Passages

- Steps to Answer Reading Questions

Reading Overview

The Reading test on the SAT is a part of your Evidence-Based Reading and Writing subscore. That score combines both the Reading and Writing and Language sections of the test. This test is 65 minutes long. The Reading Test on the ACT is scored from 1-36, is 35 minutes long, and contains the same types of questions as the SAT. Both tests include long passages (400-800 words) and paired passages on the following topics:

- Prose Fiction/Literary Narrative
- History/Humanities
- Social Science
- Natural Science

A strong vocabulary is of the utmost importance in preparing for the SAT and ACT. It is the key to both the reading and writing sections of the exam. It is almost the most boring and tedious part of SAT/ACT Preparation. I always think of studying vocabulary like doing sit ups. Sit-ups are boring and somewhat painful, but they do pay off in core strengthening. Vocabulary review will strengthen your core SAT/ACT knowledge. The SAT has been re-designed to be more similar to the ACT, and focuses on "high-utility academic words and phrases," or "Tier Two" vocabulary. Tier Two words appear in many different texts across different domains, and they often have multiple meanings, which makes understanding the context in which they are used even more important.

Good preparation will include **reading for pleasure** on your own – it is the best vocabulary tool. Four books that might interest you are:

1. *The Hot Zone* by Richard Preston
2. *Gone with the Wind* by Margaret Mitchell
3. The *Twilight* Series by Stephanie Meyer
4. The *Hunger Games* Series by Suzanne Collins

The next few pages will outline the specific strategies to answering different types of Reading questions. Your overall strategy will be:

1. Do not trust these exams. They are designed to test students' reasoning and knowledge skills so make sure that you think every question through.
2. Use a process of elimination. Look at all four of the multiple choices answers. Do not pick one until you have considered ALL four.
3. Consider each answer carefully.
4. Make a dot next to the possibly correct answers and mark all the way through the obviously incorrect answers.
5. Whittle down the answers to pick the correct one.

6. Remember that any answer you choose should be substantiated (proven true) by evidence from the passage(s). If you are unsure of an answer, do not just guess from memory—go back and look for the answer in the passage!

7. If you are having trouble, some questions ask for proof, with specific lines cited. Go to those lines, brainstorm what point they prove, and try to match it with one of the given answers.

Reading Passages

The reading sections will include both single and paired passages. On both the SAT and ACT, there are about 10 questions per passage or set of paired passages.

<u>Common Types of Reading Questions</u>:

1. **<u>Overall Meaning/Purpose</u>:** These questions will focus on the main idea of the passage. You may be asked to look at "the big picture."

2. **<u>Meaning in Context</u>:** These questions will focus on a specific idea in the passage and ask for an explanation or inference.

3. **<u>Interpretation</u>:** These questions may ask, "Why does the author say...? Or "What does the author mean by..." Students must answer based on reasoning or evidence. Make sure to look at the author's choice of words, tone and specific details supplied in the passage.

4. **<u>Tone/Mood</u>:** These questions will ask "How does the author feel about...?"

5. **<u>Synthesis</u>:** These questions will ask how ideas relate to each other in the passage.

6. **<u>Vocabulary in Context</u>:** These questions will ask about the denotations or connotations of vocabulary found in the passage. Question will often refer to specific lines in the text. Remember many words have more than one meaning; it is the meaning appropriate to the passage that you must identify.

On the next page is a specific process to answering the questions for the Reading section single and paired passages. By reading each passage one paragraph at a time and answering questions focusing on the single paragraph, you will find that you do not get bored or lose focus and forget what you have just read as easily as you normally do. One of the biggest complaints that students make about the SAT and ACT Reading sections' passages is that they are boring and easily forgettable. This process will help you to stay more active and focused.

Watch out for the following clues:

1. Words signaling a change/contrast/antonym:

- but	- yet	- since	- unless
- due to	- oddly	- because	- moreover
- curiously	- however	- although	- ironically
-uncharacteristically	- strangely	- in spite of	- nonetheless
- on the contrary	- on the other hand	- even so	- nevertheless
- while	- conversely	- despite	- not
- in contrast	- even though	- rather than	

2. Words showing comparison/synonyms:

- and	- too	- along with	- similarly
- alike/like	- plus	- also	- commonly
- or			

Steps to Answer Reading Questions:

Single Passages:

1. Always begin with the italicized print at the top of the reading; this little blurb will provide you with useful background information.

2. Begin to read the passage actively. Underline important points, make notations in the margins. Opinion and viewpoint are more important than facts.

3. Always make sure to read all of the text in each paragraph. Skimming the passage searching for answers is not a good approach. Realize that everything is important.

4. Only read one paragraph at a time.

5. After the first paragraph, answer the questions that have to do with that paragraph.

6. If the first question is one of the "whole essay" questions and you cannot answer it without reading more, skip it and go to the second question. Circle the question in your answer book and make a note on your answer sheet so that you don't skip the question or bubble incorrectly.

7. Read the question while covering up the answers to the question.

8. Before looking at the answer choices, predict a good answer.

9. Check the answer choices to see which, if any, are similar to your prediction.

10. Use the process of elimination.

11. Answer all of the questions having to do with each paragraph before moving on to the next question.

Paired Passages:

Paired passages are two reading passages that have a common theme or subject. The SAT and ACT will ask questions based on each of the passages individually and in relation to each other.

1. Read the first passage.

2. Answer questions dealing only with the first passage (probably the first three or four).

3. Read the second passage.

4. Answer questions dealing only with the second passage (usually three or four).

5. Finally, answer the questions that compare the passages (usually three or four).

Remember:

1. Do not make assumptions or judgments from your own personal experience; all answers are in the passages or may be inferred from the passages.

2. Pay attention to details.

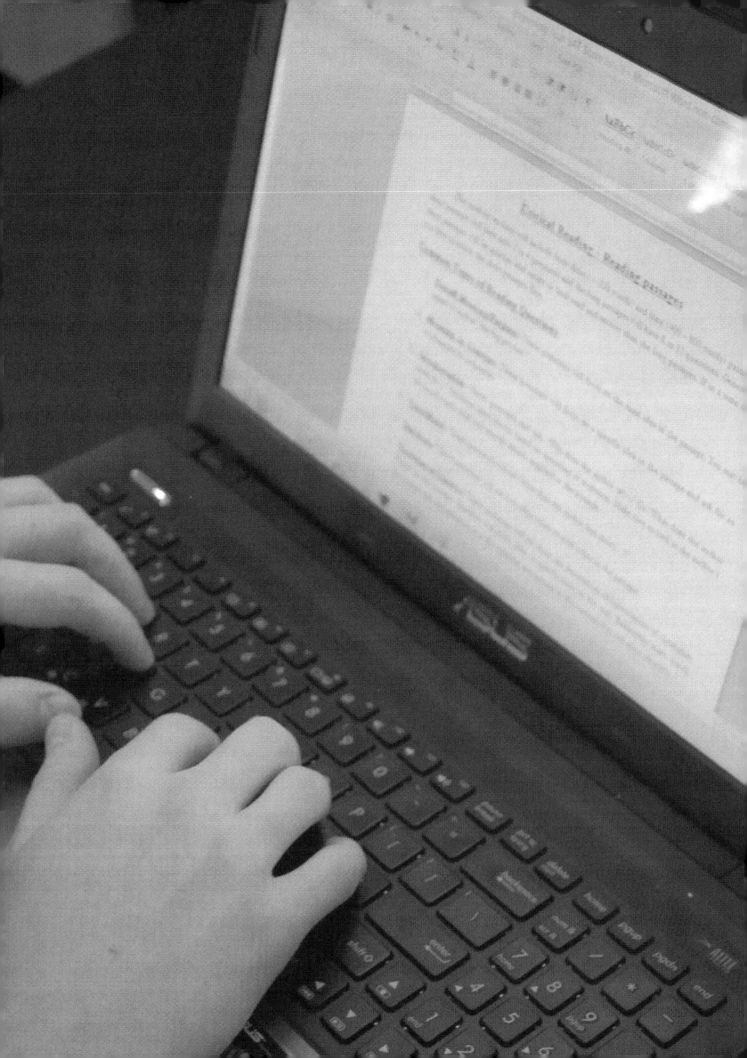

Chapter 3

Writing

In this chapter:

- Writing and Language Overview

- Multiple Choice Questions

- Grammar Rules to Know for the Exams

- SAT & ACT Essay Overview

- SAT Writing Preparation Worksheets

- SAT Essay Rubric

- ACT Writing Preparation Worksheets

- ACT Essay Rubric

- Sample Student Essays

Writing and Language Overview

The Writing and Language test is a part of your Evidence-Based Reading and Writing subscore. That score combines both the Reading and Writing and Language sections of the test. There is one 35-minute multiple-choice writing section, as well as the optional 50-minute essay. The optional essay is always the last section of the SAT.

A strong vocabulary is of the utmost importance in preparing for the SAT and ACT. It is the key to both the reading and writing sections of the exam. Studying vocabulary can seem both boring and tedious. We always think of studying vocabulary like doing sit ups. Sit-ups are boring and somewhat painful, but they do pay off in core strengthening. Vocabulary review will strengthen your core SAT/ACT knowledge. The revised SAT has been re-designed to be more like the ACT; the new SAT focuses on "high-utility academic words and phrases," or "Tier Two" vocabulary. Tier Two words appear in many different texts across different domains, and they often have multiple meanings, which makes understanding the context in which they are used even more important.

Good preparation will include **reading for pleasure** on your own – it is the best vocabulary tool. Four books that might interest you are:

1. *The Hot Zone* by Richard Preston
2. *Gone with the Wind by* Margaret Mitchell
3. The *Twilight* Series by Stephanie Meyer
4. The *Hunger Games* Series by Suzanne Collins

<u>Strategy</u>: Use a process of elimination. Always look at all of the answers listed in the multiple-choice sections. Check each answer carefully. Mark the answers that make sense and cross out the obviously bogus answers. Whittle down the answers to pick the correct one.

Multiple Choice Questions

The multiple-choice writing questions will focus on the mechanics of writing, including:
- Identifying Sentence Errors (grammar, usage, style questions).
- Improving Sentences
- Improving Paragraphs

Identifying Sentence Errors:

The multiple-choice writing questions will cover grammar, sentence structure, word choice and idiomatic expressions. The SAT and ACT will provide passages with underlined sentence parts; each sentence part will include one or more words. Each underlined portion will correspond to a question number. The first answer choice of the question (answer A) will give the "no change" option, and the next three answer choices (B, C, and D) will give options for potential corrections. You will need to spot the error, if there is one, and fill in the appropriate bubble on your answer sheet. Remember that one out of every four questions will have no error. A basic grammar rule to remember is that all sentences must have a subject and a verb and express a complete thought. More grammar and punctuation rules are covered on page 49.

Strategies to Identify Sentence Errors:
1. Read the whole sentence; listen for the mistake.
2. If the mistake is clear to you, choose the answer that fixes it. Make sure to glance at all the answers, as always!
3. If the mistake is not clear, read each underlined choice again and eliminate the choices that contain errors.
4. Make a final choice.
5. Check your final answer in the sentence.

Improving Sentences:

The Improving Sentence questions will focus on the structure of entire sentences. In this type of question, the SAT or ACT will have underlined an awkward phrase. The SAT/ACT will provide four possible answers. The first will always be a repeat of the underlined phrase. Choosing this first option means that you do not think that the sentence needs improvement. The other four options may or may not be better than the underlined phrase.

Strategies:
1. Read the whole sentence.
2. Think about the underlined phrase. Decide if it is correct.
3. In most cases, predict a good improvement.
4. Consider each of the answer choices.
5. Use the process of elimination.
6. Check your final answer in the sentence.

Improving Paragraphs:

The Improving Paragraph questions focus on improving sentence structure, word choice, and organization of the paragraph. Many times, questions will ask you to re-order the sentences to make the entire paragraph clearer. These questions may be divided into three types:
1. General paragraph organization.
2. Adding new information to the paragraph.
3. Combination of sentences.

Strategies:
1. Read the entire passage quickly for the overall idea and tone.
2. Read the question.
3. Reread the relevant portion of the paragraph (and its context which means read a line or two before and after).
4. Predict the correction.
5. Check for an error-less match.

Grammar rules to know for the exams: Most common grammar, punctuation, and syntax questions and tips

1. Know your homophones. Here are some of the most commonly confused ones to get you started:
   a. fare/fair
   b. cite/sight/site
   c. there/they're/their
   d. it's/its
   e. then/than
   f. compliment/complement
   g. your/you're
   h. rite/write/right
   i. affect/effect
   j. peak/peek/pique
   k. brake/break
   l. bear/bare
   m. allowed/aloud

2. Eliminate redundancy. Being concise is usually better. If adding words does not clarify meaning or correct a grammatical error, then do not add them—even if you think it "sounds smarter that way."

3. Keep verb tenses consistent, and use parallel structure.
   Incorrect: My dog not only lik**es** to play fetch, but also lik**ed** to chase cars.
   Incorrect: My dog not only likes play**ing** fetch, but he also likes **to chase** cars.
   Correct: My dog not only lik**es** play**ing** fetch, but he also lik**es** chas**ing** cars.

4. If a clause or phrase can be removed without changing the meaning of the sentence, then it should be surrounded by a pair of commas (or sometimes a pair of em-dashes), one at the beginning of the clause and one at the end. If removing the phrase changes the meaning, you should NOT use commas.
   Incorrect: People, who dislike music, won't enjoy rock concerts.
   Correct: People who dislike loud music won't enjoy rock concerts.
   Incorrect: I love the Harry Potter books which are full of adventure because they offer an escape from the dullness of everyday life.
   Correct: I love the Harry Potter books, which are full of adventure, because they offer an escape from the dullness of everyday life.
   Correct: I love the Harry Potter books—which are full of adventure—because they offer an escape from the dullness of everyday life.

5. When to use a comma, semicolon, colon, or em-dash
   a. Commas (,)
      i. Separate three or more items in a list.
         Example: I went to the store to buy milk, apples, bread and carrots.
      ii. Separate independent clauses (phrases that could be complete sentences) when the second clause has a FANBOYS (For, And, Nor, But, Or, Yet, So) conjunction
         Incorrect: It was raining all day, I didn't go hiking.
         Correct: It was raining all day, <u>so</u> I didn't go hiking.

        iii. Set off introductory information
            Example: During the production of the film, the star actress nearly quit.
        iv. Set off non-essential descriptive information using a **pair** of commas **(see #4)**
         v. Are used to set off a transition word (*however, therefore, for example, on the other hand,* etc.) at the beginning of a sentence. A pair of commas is used to set off a transition word in the middle of a sentence.
            Example 1: However, my sister refused to help me move the furniture.
            Example 2: My sister, however, refused to help me move the furniture.

    b. Semicolons (;)
        i. Join two independent clauses (aka complete sentences) **without** a FANBOYS conjunction. The clauses on both sides of the semicolon must both be able to work as complete, stand-alone sentences. Remember: as far as correct usage is concerned, a semicolon is interchangeable with a period.
           Incorrect: It was raining all day; <u>so</u> I didn't go hiking.
           Correct: It was raining all day; I didn't go hiking.

    c. Colons (:)
        i. Introduce lists or explanations
        ii. **Must come after an independent clause** (complete sentence). If there is not an independent clause, you cannot use a colon there.
           Incorrect: My two favorite hobbies are: skiing and reading.
           Correct: I have two favorite hobbies: skiing and reading.

    d. Em-dashes (—)
        i. Indicate a significant pause or break in thought and add emphasis. They can also be used in the same way as either a colon or a semicolon.
           Example: The message of this book is simple—study hard for your SAT.
        ii. Set off explanatory examples or information from the rest of the sentence when used in a pair **(see #4)**

6. Pay attention to subject-verb agreement and pronoun-antecedent (aka the pronoun and what it is referring to) agreement
    Incorrect: <u>People</u> often like parties because <u>he</u> gets to see <u>his</u> friends.
    Incorrect: <u>People</u> often <u>likes</u> parties because they get to see their friends.
    Correct: People often like parties because they get to see their friends.

7. Apostrophes
    a. Indicate possession: 's for singular nouns, s' for plural nouns
        Examples: Julia's phone, my friends' cars
    b. Create contractions
        Examples: who is = who's, there is = there's, it is = it's

8. Modifiers must be next to what they're modifying (avoid "dangling modifiers"). The subject of the sentence <u>must</u> immediately follow the modifier. Think: what or whom is being described? Does the wording of the sentence make that clear?
    Incorrect: Having arrived late for class, <u>a written excuse</u> was needed.
    Correct: Having arrived late for class, <u>the student</u> needed a written excuse.

9. Which vs. that: Which one is correct? Do I need a comma?
   a. If you are using "which," you need to use a comma because "which" is used to introduce non-essential descriptive information.
   Example: My bike, which has a flat tire, is in the garage.
   This sentence simply describes the bike and identifies its location; there's no implication that the speaker owns more than one bike.
   b. If you are using "that," you are describing and defining the noun that comes before it, and introducing essential information that cannot be separated from that noun. Therefore, you should not use a comma.
   Example: My bike that has a flat tire is in the garage.
   This sentence implies that the speaker has more than one bike, and the one with a broken wheel is in the garage.

10. Run-on sentences and sentence fragments
    a. Make sure the sentence has a subject, a verb, expresses a complete thought, and makes sense on its own. This is a complete sentence, or an **independent clause**. If the sentence has two independent clauses, you can join them with a comma and a FANBOYS conjunction **(see 5.a.ii)**. Alternatively, you can split the two clauses with either a period or a semicolon **(see 5.b)**.
    Incorrect: I love to write short stories I would write one every day if I had the time.
    Correct: I love to write short stories, and I would write one every day if I had the time.
    Correct: I love to write short stories; I would write one every day if I had the time.
    Correct: I love to write short stories. I would write one every day if I had the time.
    b. If a clause lacks a subject, verb, or does not make sense on its own, then it is incorrect and considered a sentence fragment, and is not a complete sentence. It must either be attached to an independent clause with a comma, or be corrected in such a way that it becomes an independent clause.
    Incorrect: Because his car was in the shop.
    Correct: Because his car was in the shop, he had to take the bus to work.
    Correct: He had to take the bus to work because his car was in the shop.

SAT & ACT Essay Overview

The SAT Essay

The Redesigned SAT Essay is a completely different task with completely different requirements and grading criteria from the old SAT Essay. Now, instead of writing about their opinion on a topic, students are asked to read a passage and explain how the author of that passage builds his or her argument.

These changes were made in order to better measure students' reading comprehension and analysis skills, and their ability to support their points with evidence and nuanced thinking. The SAT Essay is a lot like a typical college writing assignment in which you're asked to analyze a text. You will be given an essay or transcription of a speech from a historical thinker, always from a published work. By testing a student's ability to write in this way, the SAT seeks to evaluate how well the student will do on college-level writing assignments.

What You'll Do

- Read a passage 500-1000 words (1-2 pages).
- Explain how the author builds an argument to persuade an audience, and support your explanation with evidence from the passage.
- Analytical writing, not opinion-based.
- Graded on: Reading, Analysis, Writing.
- 50 minutes

The ACT Writing Test

In the new ACT Writing Test, students are also tested on their analytical writing ability. However, unlike the SAT essay, in this case they are asked to write a persuasive essay requiring them to take a position on an issue. Students are given a short (~100 word) overview of an issue, followed by three different perspectives on that issue. They are then asked to choose their own perspective on the issue and discuss the relationship between the perspective they chose and the other given perspectives.

What You'll Do

- 100 words overview, three short opinions on a continuum
- Analyze and relate the three different perspectives on a specific issue to each other and to your own opinion.
- Graded on: Ideas and Analysis, Development and Support, Organization. Language Use and Conventions.
- 40 minutes

Scoring

SAT: scored from 2-8 in each of the three categories listed above; the scores are then added for a final score out of 24.

ACT: scored from 2-12 in each of the four categories listed above; the scores are then averaged for a final score out of 12.

Similarities
- Both are optional additions to the main exam, and are taken after completing the other four sections.
- Both tests require critical analysis.
- Both tests score students on organization and technical writing skills.

Differences
- SAT: requires literary analysis of a text.
- ACT: requires students to construct logical arguments and analyze how multiple viewpoints relate.
- SAT: not opinion-based writing.
- ACT: opinion-based writing.
- SAT: students use evidence found in the passage.
- ACT: students must come up with their own evidence.

Learning to work on each

Both essays require you to have a deep understanding of how arguments are constructed. In the SAT, you will be analyzing how an author or historical figure does this, and in the ACT you will be constructing an argument of your own.

The purpose of the following pages is to teach you how to write successful SAT and ACT essays. For your convenience, we have broken down these essays for you step-by-step and paragraph-by-paragraph. There were no published rubrics for the essays available, so we have created our own, which you will find on pages 68 and 85.

SAT Writing Preparation for the Re-designed SAT - Overview

The purpose of the 50-minute optional SAT Essay is for the College Board to measure each student's ability to understand and analyze complex college-level passages and ideas. According to the College Board, the organization that writes and administers the r-SAT Exam (and other exams including Advanced Placement and SAT Subject Exams), *the essay gives you an opportunity to show how effectively you can read and comprehend a passage and write an essay analyzing the passage. In your essay, you should demonstrate that you have read the passage carefully, present a clear and logical analysis, and use language precisely.*

In this essay, the College Board is specifically evaluating your reading, reasoning and writing skills. The College Board has made it very clear that the graders have absolutely NO interest in your opinion on the passage's topic or validity. In fact, your score will be lowered if you offer an opinion; the SAT essay is supposed to be a completely objective literary analysis on your part.

Two readers will score each r-SAT essay on a scale of 1-12 (up to four points for each section detailed below). The two readers' scores are added together. Essay scores range from 2-24 points. On www.CollegeBoard.com, the College Board describes its detailed grading basis (quoted below):

Reading: A successful essay shows that you understood the passage, including the interplay of central ideas and important details. It also shows an effective use of textual evidence.

Analysis: A successful essay shows your understanding of how the author builds an argument by:
- Examining the author's use of evidence, reasoning, and other stylistic and persuasive techniques
- Supporting and developing claims with well-chosen evidence from the passage

Writing: A successful essay is focused, organized, and precise, with an appropriate style and tone that varies sentence structure and follows the conventions of standard written English.

As the College Board's scoring is provided in a narrative format, we, at Professional Tutoring, created a detailed rubric to help our students understand this complex essay's requirements (see page 68).

The question always arises as to the necessity of taking this optional essay. Professional Tutoring recommends that ALL students prepare for and take the r-SAT essay. First, this essay provides an excellent opportunity to learn how to write a college-level analytical essay. The r-SAT essay will open your eyes to complex literary analysis and upper level writing. But, you may argue, not all schools require the r-SAT essay for admission. This is true. But, and this is a big but, most (really all) juniors do not identify EVERY college on their application list before they take the r-SAT Exam. What happens to students who elect not to complete the SAT essay and later want to consider applying to a school which recommends or requires the essay? Our advice: extra preparation can ONLY benefit students. Furthermore, some colleges download the SAT essay to compare it to a student's submitted admissions essays or to evaluate a student's writing ability.

In the pages following, you will find worksheets to refresh your memory on evidence-based reading, passage analysis, reasoning methods and literary techniques. We have also included worksheets to help you lay out your five-paragraph essay and a scoring rubric.

Part I: Critical Thinking and Writing Preparation

A. Analysis:

1. What is passage-based analysis?

_____

_____

_____

2. What are the goals of passage-based analysis? Why?

_____

_____

_____

B. Types of Evidence:

The SAT repeatedly emphasizes "command of evidence." This is your ability to understand and utilize the evidence effectively. The author of the essay will provide factual evidence to support his/her argument and your job is to analyze the effectiveness of their argument. What are different types of evidence that he or she could use? Is one type of evidence more credible than others? Be sure the evidence you use in your writing is textual only and supports your thesis.

1. Facts:

_____

_____

Example: _____

2. Documentation (letters, diaries, historical documents, laws, etc.):

_____

_____

Example: _____

3. Expert Testimony:

_____

_____

Example: _____

4. Interview:

_____

_____

Example: _____

5. Quote:

_____

_____

Example: _____

6. Statistics:

_____

_____

Example: _____

7. Surveys:

_____

_____

Example: _____

8. Graphs/Charts:

_____

_____

Example: _____

9. Personal Experience:

_____

_____

Example: _____

C. Reasoning

In order to understand and draw conclusions about the facts provided by the author, students must use reasoning skills. Occasionally, you may have to make assumptions of an author's intent if it is not clearly stated. You must also use reasoning in order to decide if evidence strengthens or weakens the author's argument. There are two types of reasoning: inductive and deductive. Define below:

Deductive: _____

Inductive: _____

D. Persuasive Techniques:

1. Who first defined "Persuasive Techniques"?

_____

2. Define, explain, and provide an example of each. Think about how each one strengthens an argument.

a. Pathos:

_____

_____

b. Logos:

_____

_____

c. Ethos: _____

_____

E. Logical Sequencing

In order for your essay to be persuasive and build your argument, you must use powerful language and logically sequence your ideas.

1. What does logical sequencing in creating a written argument mean to you?

_____

_____

F. Literary Devices:

Explain the following literary devices and their purpose in expository writing:

1. Voice:

_____

_____

Purpose: _____

2. Diction:

_____

_____

Types of Diction:_____

Purpose:_____

3. Rhetoric:

_____

_____

Purpose: _____

4. Repetition:

_____

_____

Purpose: _____

5. Metaphor:

_____

_____

Purpose: _____

6. Anecdote:

_____

_____

Purpose: _____

7. Hyperbole:

_____

_____

Purpose: _____

8. Juxtaposition:

_____

_____

Purpose: _____

9. Appeal to Emotion:

_____

_____

Purpose: _____

Part II: Understanding the Prompt

Redesigned SAT Essay Requirements:

As you read the passage below, consider how the author uses:

- Evidence, such as facts or examples, to support claims.
- Reasoning to develop ideas and to connect claims and evidence.
- Stylistic or persuasive elements, such as word choice or appeals to emotion, to add power to the ideas expressed.

General Redesigned SAT Prompt:

Write an essay in which you explain how the author builds an argument to persuade his audience of his premise. In your essay, analyze how the author uses one or more of the features in the directions that precede the passage (or features of your own choice) to strengthen the logic and persuasiveness of his argument. Be sure that your analysis focuses on the most relevant features of the passage.

Your essay should not explain whether you agree with the author's claims, but rather explain how the author builds an argument to persuade his audience.

** Professional Tutoring recommends that you evaluate all three suggested components:

- Use of evidence
- Reasoning (ethos, pathos, logos)
- Literary Devices

Preparing to write:

1. In your own words, explain what the SAT is asking you to do in your 50-minute essay.

_____

_____

_____

_____

_____

_____

Part III: Writing – Steps to Success

1. Remember the point of this essay. You are <u>analyzing</u> the author's argument. Use your command of evidence and make sure it's logically sequenced.

2. Carefully read and engage with the SAT's offered passage:
    *   What is the author discussing/arguing?
    *   Do you believe that the author has written effectively?
    *   Did you come away with any thoughts or feelings?
    *   Is there a point that resonates with or affected you? Why? How?
    *   Underline key points and annotate text

3. Before you outline, review the definition of *logical sequencing* (page 57). Putting your thoughts and ideas into a logical order so that you can persuade your reader of your argument is just as important as your argument and evidence. This includes grouping evidence with each segment of your argument, as opposed to toggling back and forth between your points.

4. Create a five-paragraph outline as per these worksheets.

5. Do NOT even think about writing before taking at least 5-10 minutes to complete steps 2, 3 and 4.

6. Timing:

5 minutes:	Reading and annotating
5 minutes:	Outlining with examples
35 minutes:	Write your essay
5 minutes:	Proofread

7. Create a five-paragraph outline, as per these worksheets
8. Try to write your essay in the approximately 35 minutes you would have after outlining. Make sure to leave time to proofread.

9. As you write, keep the following in mind:
    *   Write formally – 5 paragraphs, academic diction, no contractions, no first or second person.
    *   Use academic vocabulary correctly; use words that you know well. Advanced vocabulary sounds very stilted (awkward) when not used correctly.
    *   Use transitional sentences between paragraphs as you change from one point to the next. This will help readers follow your arguments.
    *   When using quotes, feel free to shorten them by using only the parts that you need. You may separate quotes with "..."

10. Re-read what you wrote. Does it effectively answer the questions? Is it logically sequenced? Was your evidence strictly textual and supportive of your thesis? Does it have the tone you wanted to convey? Is it clearly written? Check for grammatical and spelling errors.

11. Score yourself using the Professional Tutoring SAT Essay Rubric on page 68.

Sample SAT Passages for Analysis

Preamble to the United States Constitution

The Preamble to the Constitution is an introductory, succinct statement of the principles at work in the full Constitution.

We the people of the United States, in order to form a more perfect union, establish justice, insure domestic tranquility, provide for the common defense, promote the general welfare, and secure the blessings of liberty to ourselves and our posterity, do ordain and establish this Constitution for the United States of America.

Preamble to the Declaration of Independence

IN CONGRESS, July 4, 1776.

The unanimous Declaration of the thirteen united States of America,

When in the Course of human events, it becomes necessary for one people to dissolve the political bands which have connected them with another, and to assume among the powers of the earth, the separate and equal station to which the Laws of Nature and of Nature's God entitle them, a decent respect to the opinions of mankind requires that they should declare the causes which impel them to the separation.

We hold these truths to be self-evident, that all men are created equal, that they are endowed by their Creator with certain unalienable Rights, that among these are Life, Liberty and the pursuit of Happiness.--That to secure these rights, Governments are instituted among Men, deriving their just powers from the consent of the governed, --That whenever any Form of Government becomes destructive of these ends, it is the Right of the People to alter or to abolish it, and to institute new Government, laying its foundation on such principles and organizing its powers in such form, as to them shall seem most likely to effect their Safety and Happiness. Prudence, indeed, will dictate that Governments long established should not be changed for light and transient causes; and accordingly all experience hath shewn, that mankind are more disposed to suffer, while evils are sufferable, than to right themselves by abolishing the forms to which they are accustomed. But when a long train of abuses and usurpations, pursuing invariably the same Object evinces a design to reduce them under absolute Despotism, it is their right, it is their duty, to throw off such Government, and to provide new Guards for their future security.--Such has been the patient sufferance of these Colonies; and such is now the necessity which constrains them to alter their former Systems of Government. The history of the present King of Great Britain is a history of repeated injuries and usurpations, all having in direct object the establishment of an absolute Tyranny over these States. To prove this, let Facts be submitted to a candid world.

Martin Luther King's "I Have a Dream" Speech, delivered August 28, 1963 (excerpt)

I am happy to join with you today in what will go down in history as the greatest demonstration for freedom in the history of our nation.

Five score years ago, a great American, in whose symbolic shadow we stand today, signed the Emancipation Proclamation. This momentous decree came as a great beacon light of hope to millions of Negro slaves who had been seared in the flames of withering injustice. It came as a joyous daybreak to end the long night of captivity.

But one hundred years later, the Negro still is not free. One hundred years later, the life of the Negro is still sadly crippled by the manacles of segregation and the chains of discrimination. One hundred years later, the Negro lives on a lonely island of poverty in the midst of a vast ocean of material prosperity. One hundred years later, the Negro is still languished in the corners of American society and finds himself in exile in his own land. So we have come here today to dramatize a shameful condition.

In a sense we've come to our nation's Capital to cash a check. When the architects of our republic wrote the magnificent words of the Constitution and the Declaration of Independence, they were signing a promissory note to which every American was to fall heir.

This note was a promise that all men, yes, black men as well as white men, would be guaranteed the unalienable rights of life, liberty, and the pursuit of happiness.

It is obvious today that America has defaulted on this promissory note insofar as her citizens of color are concerned. Instead of honoring this sacred obligation, America has given the Negro people a bad check; a check which has come back marked "insufficient funds."

But we refuse to believe that the bank of justice is bankrupt. We refuse to believe that there are insufficient funds in the great vaults of opportunity of this nation. So we have come to cash this check- a check that will give us upon demand the riches of freedom and the security of justice.

We have also come to this hallowed spot to remind America of the fierce urgency of now. This is no time to engage in the luxury of cooling off or to take the tranquilizing drug of gradualism...

This will be the day when all of God's children will be able to sing with new meaning, "My country 'tis of thee, sweet land of liberty, of thee I sing. Land where my fathers died, land of the Pilgrims' pride, from every mountainside, let freedom ring."

And if America is to be a great nation, this must become true. So let freedom ring from the prodigious hilltops of New Hampshire. Let freedom ring from the mighty mountains of New York. Let freedom ring from the heightening Alleghenies of Pennsylvania.

Let freedom ring from the snow-capped Rockies of Colorado. Let freedom ring from the curvaceous slopes of California. But not only that; let freedom ring from the Stone Mountain of Georgia. Let freedom ring from Lookout Mountain of Tennessee.

Let freedom ring from every hill and molehill of Mississippi. From every mountainside, let freedom ring.

And when this happens, and when we allow freedom ring, when we let it ring from every village and every hamlet, from every state and every city, we will be able to speed up that day when all of God's children, black men and white men, Jews and gentiles, Protestants and Catholics, will be able to join hands and sing in the words of the old Negro spiritual, "Free at last! Free at last! Thank God Almighty, we are free at last!"

Part IV- Analysis – Outlining with Notes

Assignment: Using 50 minutes and up to four sides of lined paper, write an essay in which you explain how the author builds an argument to persuade his audience of his premise. In your essay, analyze how the author uses one or more of the features in the directions that precede the passage (or features of your own choice) to strengthen the logic and persuasiveness of his argument. Be sure that your analysis focuses on the most relevant features of the passage.

Your essay should not explain whether you agree with the author's claims, but rather explain how the author builds an argument to persuade his audience.

Passage: CB Test # _____, Constitution, Declaration of Independence, MLK Speech (Circle one)

Paragraph 1: Introduction: In your introduction, include a clear beginning. In 5-7 sentences, you should summarize the author's argument to prove that you have understood the passage. The College Board allocates eight of 24 points to evaluating the students' understanding of the passage. Use specific examples! At the end of the introduction, you will want to clearly state that in the following essay, you will evaluate the author's evidence, reasoning and literary devices; you may mention that you will evaluate evidence in the second paragraph, reasoning in the third and literary devices in the fourth. This sentence will transition your writing to paragraph two and support your reader in following your logic.

_____

_____

_____

_____

_____

_____

_____

_____

_____

Paragraph 2: Evidence: In this paragraph, examine any evidence that the author uses, such as facts or examples, to support his or her claim. Find at least two data points from the author and underline them in your SAT book. The paragraph can look at instances in which the evidence was particularly effective, or conversely, when it was not effective. Cite specific evidence. You may also focus on how the author uses the evidence. For example, was one type of evidence used too frequently? Should another have been used more? How did the author build the argument? Use specific examples from the text.

_____

_____

_____

_____

_____

_____

Paragraph 3: Reasoning: In this paragraph, analyze the author's logic and argument. This can include examining how an author does (or does not) use clear, logical reasoning to draw a connection between a claim and the evidence. It can also look at the impact of the author's message. Example: How did the results of the survey allow the author to make inferences about the topic? How did it further prove his point or enhance his argument? Could it have viewed another way by an opposing set of eyes? Discuss ethos, pathos, logos.

_____

_____

_____

_____

_____

_____

Paragraph 4: Literary Devices: There are a number of literary and stylistic devices and techniques that authors use to convey their messages, strengthen their argument or connect with the reader. These can be, but are not limited to, word choice, rhetoric, tone, and internal organizational pattern. Determine which are used and analyze the effectiveness of those present in the passage.

_____

_____

_____

_____

_____

_____

_____

_____

Paragraph 5: Conclusion: In the conclusion, it is important to have a sense of completeness. Make sure to avoid introducing new ideas. Instead, focus on reiterating the main points and thesis – reiterating your three main points: evidence, reasoning skills (ethos, pathos, logos) and literary devices.

_____

_____

_____

_____

_____

_____

_____

Part V- Self-Evaluation

In general, how did you do? _____

_____

Did you summarize the passage with 2-4 data points to prove your understanding in the first paragraph of your essay?

_____

Did you answer the prompt? Were you able to find two examples of evidence, reasoning and literary devices? Re-read and check!

Evidence: _____

_____

Reasoning: _____

_____

Literary Devices: _____

_____

Most importantly, did you sequence your arguments in order? Outline your main points below:

1. _____

2. _____

3. _____

4. _____

Score yourself with the Professional Tutoring r-SAT Essay Rubric on the following two pages.

Professional Tutoring SAT Essay Grading Rubric

Name:	Date:		
SAT Test #:	ID Number:		
Passage:			

Grading Category		Yes?	Comments
Reading (8 point total)			
Passage Context			
Cite the passage's author			
Cite the year, time frame, circumstances of the era			
Purpose of the text			
Discuss the tone of the text			
Is the author uniquely qualified to write this passage?			
Does this passage have an impact: global, national, local			
Discuss the authors reliance on opinion, facts, research emotions			
Summarize the text: 2 data points, 2 arguments			
Scoring Basis			
Demonstrate an understanding of the passage as a whole			
Demonstrate an understanding of author's central idea and details			
Interprets beyond recapping ideas			
Make skillful use of author's textual evidence			
READING SCORE			/8
Passage Analysis (8 points total)			
Introduction to Passage Analysis - Body paragraphs of essay			
Evaluate the author's thesis			
Introduce your evaluation of author's success			
Introduce pathos to invoke an emotional response in reader			
Introduce logos to support own claim with evidence			
Introduce ethos to build credibility and respect from reader			
Analysis of Evidence			
Cite two specific points of evidence that author uses			
Identify type of evidence, e.g. primary/secondary research, quotes, data			
Does the author use personal experience in addition/instead of data?			
Analyze author's choice of factual evidence			
Analyze credibility of author's evidence			
Evaluation of Author's Reasoning Ability			
Answer specifically - is author's reasoning persuasive and effective?			
Discuss ethos, logos, pathos explicitly			
Provide two examples of how author uses data to infer/create arguments			
Descibe two of the author's reasoning/argument skills			
Analyze effectiveness of author's argument			
Focus on features of text that are relevant to argument			

Evaluation of Use of Literary Devices		
Introduce two literary devices used by the author		
Explain why the author used these specific literary devices		
Analyze effectiveness of these literary devices in making argument		
Conclusion of Author's Reasoning Ability		
Return to two major evidentiary points		
Include evidence analysis		
Include reasoning evaluation		
Include literary devices		
Conclude with evaluation of overall effectiveness - well done or no?		
PASSAGE ANALYSIS SCORE		__/8
Writing (8 points total)		
5 Paragraphs		
Clear Introduction		
3 Body Paragraphs with separate topics		
Clear Conclusion		
Transitional sentences between each paragraph		
The examples follow the order in the introduction		
Uses present verb tense for literature		
Uses past tense for history		
Uses consistent verb tense for argument		
Uses parallelism		
Does not use contractions		
Does not use second person		
Objective tone and formal style		
Mostly active, minimal passive voice		
Varies sentence structure		
Uses correct spelling		
Uses punctuation correctly		
Subjects and verbs agree		
Nouns/Subject and pronouns agree		
Strong grasp of words' denotation/connotation		
Mature vocabulary		
Vocabulary does not "overwhelm" the essay		
Uses advanced techniques, e.g. "Rule of Three"		
Student uses figurative language to strengthen argument		
Demonstrates proofreading		
WRITING SCORE		__/8
Essay Grade (out of 24 possible points)		
Additional Comments		

2016 Writing Preparation for the "Enhanced" ACT Essay - Overview

While the purpose of the ACT Essay is similar to that of the SAT Essay, to measure a student's ability to write analytically and argumentatively, the ACT essay does not require the extensive literary analysis of the SAT. Instead the ACT will evaluate your ability to understand, analyze AND relate three different perspectives on a specific issue to each other and to your specific opinion. The perspectives will include a far left, middle of the road and far right opinion on a continuum. The ACT essay asks you to take a stance on the issue outlined in the prompt (~100 words) and compare your perspective to the three different views (~ 30 words per perspective) offered with the prompt. Www.ACT.org states that the new ACT Essay requires "critical engagement" and "asks students to develop an argument that puts their own perspective in dialogue with [perspectives of] others."

Graders will evaluate your writing on the four domains listed below (paraphrased from www.ACT.org).

Domain (Grading Criteria)	Students' Writing Goal
Ideas and Analysis:	- Demonstrate understanding of multiple perspectives - Generate ideas, reasoning to support various perspectives including the student's viewpoint

Development and Support:	- Clear discussion of ideas, rationale and argument
	- Student guides the reader through his/her argument with examples to support points
	- Student will evaluate the implications/consequences of his/her argument or proposed changes
	** From Professional Tutoring: You must
	    - Refute the authors' argument(s)
	    - Establish and refute counterarguments
	    - Relate each of the three examples to your position

Organization:	- Ideas are organized logically with clarity and purpose - Logical ordering guides the reader through the student's discussion.
Language Use and Conventions:	- Demonstrate writing ability through the correct usage of grammar, syntax, word usage, and mechanics - Students will use an appropriate, understandable tone

Since not all students opt to complete the ACT essay, your essay score will be separate from your ACT Composite Score. You will receive a total of five scores for this test: a score in each of the four domains listed above, which are then averaged together to generate a single subject-level writing score. Each of your domain scores will range from 2-12, as will your total essay score.

To provide students with more detailed guidance, Professional Tutoring developed an ACT Essay Scoring Rubric (provided later in this chapter).

Part I: Critical Thinking and Writing Preparation

For the SAT essay, you learned about the different literary devices, evidence, and persuasive techniques that writers use to make their writing more persuasive. In this essay, instead of analyzing these techniques, you will be putting them into practice in order to strengthen your own writing and convince the reader of your point of view. Please use the questions on the page below to gather your thoughts for the ACT essay.

A. Analytical and Writing Skills:

1. Critical Reasoning:

_____

_____

Examples: _____

_____

_____

2. Refutation:

_____

_____

Purpose and Examples:

_____

_____

_____

3. Academic Argument:

_____

_____

Examples: _____

_____

_____

4. Academic Counterargument:

_____

_____

Examples: _____

_____

_____

5. Spectrum of Ideas:

_____

_____

_____

Examples: _____

_____

_____

6. Sequencing of Arguments:

_____

_____

Examples: _____

_____

_____

B. Types of Evidence:

In the ACT essay, you will provide factual evidence to support your argument. What are different types of evidence that you could use? Is one type of evidence more credible than others? Think about where you would find this evidence.

1. What is the purpose of using evidence in an academic essay?

_____

_____

_____

2. Direct Quotes:

_____

_____

Purpose in an argument essay: _____

_____

3. Academic Examples: History, Literature, Science, Current Events:

_____

_____

_____

Examples, familiar to you:

_____

_____

_____

_____

How could you use these examples?

_____

_____

_____

C. Writing Skills

Logical Sequencing

In order for your essay to be persuasive and build your argument, you must use powerful language and logically sequence your ideas.

1. What does logical sequencing in creating a written argument mean to you? Why do you use it?

_____

_____

Part II: Unpacking the Prompt

General Redesigned ACT Prompt:

Write a unified, coherent essay in which you evaluate multiple perspectives on the given topic. In your essay, be sure to:
1. Analyze and evaluate the perspectives given
2. State and develop your own perspective on the issue
3. Explain the relationship between your perspective and those given.

Your perspective may be in full agreement with any of the others, in partial agreement, or wholly different. Whatever the case, support your ideas with logical reasoning and detailed, persuasive examples.

The ACT gives you these further instructions/hints on the pages provided for your prewriting:

Planning Your Essay

Your work on these prewriting pages will not be scored.

Use the space below and on the back cover to generate ideas and plan your essay. You may wish to consider the following as you think critically about the task:

Significance of the overview:
- Historical
- Cultural
- Literary
- Science
- Current Events

Strengths and weaknesses of the three given perspectives
- What insights do they offer, and what do they fail to consider?
- Why might they be persuasive to others, or why might they fail to persuade?

Your own knowledge experience and values
- What is your perspective on this issue, and what are its strengths and weaknesses?
- How will you support your perspective in your essay?

Preparing to write:

In your own words, explain what the ACT is asking you to do in your 40-minute essay.

_____

_____

_____

Part III: Writing – Steps to Success

1. Carefully read the prompt and all three of the given perspectives. It is important that you fully understand what all three of the perspectives are arguing.

2. Evaluate the overview.
   - What is the general topic?
   - Jot down some facts about the topic in general. What is the history of this issue? Make connections: culture, economics, sociology, psychology, personal experience. This will become your introduction and carry you through the essay. You will also tie the essay together in your conclusion and return to these details.

3. Re-read the three perspectives to create your essay argument and outline.
   - Lay out the three arguments in a logical sequence from left to right from one extreme to the other, along a spectrum.
   - Jot down positive and negative points for each perspective.
   - Jot down an argument (you may paraphrase the author's argument) and counterargument for each example (you must have your own).
   - Evaluate: Does one position resonate the most with you?
   - Which position would be the easiest for you to support? This is the one which you will defend in your essay.
   - Why does your chosen perspective make more sense than the others?
   - Brainstorm evidence supporting your position. Although the ACT does not deduct points for factually inaccurate information, do not blatantly falsify your data points.
   - Brainstorm counterarguments to your position and your own refutations of these counterarguments.

4. Consider the tone you want to convey - you are trying to persuade your reader that your opinion is the right one, so it's ok to be more passionate and perhaps take a slightly less formal tone.

5. Do NOT even think about writing before taking at least five minutes to complete steps 1, 2, and 3.

6. Timing: 5 minutes: Brainstorm ideas and evidence, outline
              30 minutes: Write your essay
              5 minutes: Proofread

7. Write your thesis. You should state exactly what position you are arguing and which perspectives you agree/disagree with.

8. Create a five-paragraph outline, as per these worksheets.

9. Try to write your essay in the approximately 30 minutes you will have after the outlining. Make sure to leave time to proofread.

10. As you write, keep the following in mind:
   - Write formally – Five paragraphs, academic diction, no contractions, no second person and minimal first person.
   - Use academic vocabulary correctly; use words that you know well. Advanced vocabulary sounds very stilted (awkward) when not used correctly.
   - Use transitional sentences between paragraphs as you change from one point to the next. This will help readers follow your arguments.
   - Remember: If your evidence does not clearly and directly relate to your thesis, you should not include it in your essay.

11. Re-read what you have written. Does it effectively answer the questions? Is it logically sequenced? Does your evidence strongly and directly support your thesis and arguments? Does it have the tone you wanted to convey? Is it clearly written? Check for grammatical and spelling errors.

12. Score yourself using the Professional Tutoring ACT Essay Rubric on page 85.

Sample ACT Passages for Analysis

I.   Liberal Arts

For thousands of years, educated people have studied the liberal arts as part of an academic curriculum. This curriculum has included areas of study such as history, religion, philosophy, literature, music, art, and foreign and ancient languages. During this time, it was thought that a well-rounded person must be fluent in these subjects and that humans had much to learn from the arts and previous societies. However, in the twenty-first century, some people argue that the liberal arts are no longer necessary because our society's culture is now based upon technological and business advancements. The liberal arts are sometimes seen as suitable for those with money and time to spare, but for people who want to study those subjects that will help them succeed and thrive in our modern economy, they are seen as a dalliance or something to study in free time, but not worthy of study as careers or even as supports to other careers.

Read and carefully consider these perspectives. Each suggests a way of thinking about the changing value of the liberal arts in our culture.

Perspective One	Perspective Two	Perspective Three
The liberal arts have lost their value in our technology-based society and should not be required in an academic curriculum. Areas of study need to be relevant and lead to an individual obtaining a job.	Some of the liberal arts are important and should be studied. We need to know history and how to effectively read and write, but otherwise, the liberal arts are too expensive to study if they do not lead to a job.	The liberal arts allow us to experience and understand our human condition and are vital to being a well-rounded person and society.

Essay Task
Write a unified, coherent essay in which you evaluate multiple perspectives on the changing value of the liberal arts in our society. In your essay, be sure to: • Analyze and evaluate the perspectives given   • State and develop your own perspective on the issue   • Explain the relationships between your perspective and those given   Your perspective may be in full agreement with any of the others, in partial agreement, or wholly different. Whatever the case, support your ideas with logical reasoning and detailed, persuasive examples.

II.   Social Media

Social media is now so ubiquitous that it is an everyday part of many Americans' lives, consuming many hours a day for some people. As social media has increased our ability to connect with others who share our lives and our interests, it has also resulted in unintended negative consequences such as cyberbullying, attention issues, and "wasted" time. Some might say that the ability to stay in touch with those far away and to share our interests with the entire world offset the negatives, but others might say that we are too connected and that social media is impacting our ability to interact with those people right in front of us. It is clear that social media has dramatically changed our lives, and we need to consider its benefits as well as its disadvantages.

Read and carefully consider these perspectives. Each suggests a way of thinking about the impact of social media on our lives.

Perspective One	Perspective Two	Perspective Three
Social media has increased our ability to interact with our family and friends as well as others who share our interests.	Social media has ruined personal relationships and leads to shallow relationships. It takes people away from socializing in person and instead allows them to connect with others behind a computer screen.	Social media gives everyone a voice and allows shy, introverted people to participate in social rituals and express themselves. It also allows for the creation of political movements and community organizing.

Essay Task

Write a unified, coherent essay in which you evaluate multiple perspectives on the impact of social media on our lives. In your essay, be sure to:

- Analyze and evaluate the perspectives given
- State and develop your own perspective on the issue
- Explain the relationships between your perspective and those given

Your perspective may be in full agreement with any of the others, in partial agreement, or wholly different. Whatever the case, support your ideas with logical reasoning and detailed, persuasive examples.

Part IV - Analysis – Outlining

In the "enhanced" ACT essay, brainstorming and outlining is possibly the most important step of your writing process. You are not just being graded on your writing ability, but also on the nuance, depth, and insight of your ideas. Sound reasoning that considers **all** of the perspectives is key. The organizational structure of your essay should enhance the flow of your essay, and aid the reader in following the logic of your arguments.

Recommended ACT Essay Outline:

1. Introduction: Overview of issue, cite history, literature, science, current events, etc. Why is this background important? Transition to modern era and address all three perspectives briefly. End with your thesis (your position).

2. Body Paragraph 1:   Transition into the argument with which you disagree most strongly.   Give the text's example or another example and address why you disagree.

3. Body Paragraph 2:   Transition into the next argument with which you disagree. Address the text's example or other example and why you disagree.

4. Body Paragraph 3:   Transition into the argument with which you agree. State the text's argument, give an example, and explain why you agree. Also present a counterargument to your position and refute it to show why your position is more valid.

5. Conclusion: Return to your central argument, re-stating the overview from your introduction.

Prompt:

Introduction: In your introduction, include a clear beginning that addresses the background or context of the issue. You may include a sentence or two using points from history, literature, current events, science, etc.

_____

_____

_____

Transition into the modern era. How does the issue present itself today and how is it relevant to modern life?

_____

_____

Address all three perspectives briefly and how they relate to our modern era:

_____

_____

_____

Transition into and state your thesis (your position on the issue):

_____

_____

_____

Body Paragraph 1: In this paragraph you will address the issue with which you disagree most strongly.

Transition into and state the text's argument:

_____

_____

Give an example from the given perspective or from current events (you should use a paraphrase or direct quote if relevant and possible):

_____

_____

Now counter the text's argument and explain why you disagree with it:

_____

_____

Body Paragraph 2: In this paragraph you will address the other argument with which you disagree.

Transition into and state the text's argument:

_____

_____

Give an example from the author's perspective or from current events (you should use a paraphrase or direct quote if relevant and possible):

_____

_____

Now counter the text's argument and explain why you disagree with it:

_____

_____

_____

Body Paragraph 3: In this paragraph you will summarize and explain your perspective in detail.

Transition into and state the text's argument:

_____

_____

Give an example from the text's perspective or from current events (you should use a paraphrase or direct quote if relevant and possible):

_____

_____

Explain why you agree with this position:

_____

_____

Explain the counterargument (why someone might disagree with your position):

_____

_____

Refute the counterargument (why your position is better):

_____

_____

Paragraph 5: Conclusion: In the conclusion, it is important to have a sense of completeness. Make sure to avoid introducing new ideas. Instead, focus on reiterating the main points and thesis. Re-state your thesis.

_____

_____

_____

_____

Part V- Self-Evaluation

In general, how did you do?

_____

_____

Introduction: Did you give background/context and address the modern implications of this issue? Yes or No (circle). Did you briefly state all three perspectives and clearly state your position? Yes or No (circle)

First body paragraph: Did you address the perspective with which you most strongly disagree by presenting the argument, giving an example, and countering the argument? Yes or No (circle). Describe below.

Perspective:
_____

Example:
_____

Counterargument:
_____

Second body paragraph: Did you address the second perspective with which you disagree by presenting the argument, giving an example, and countering the argument? Yes or No (circle). Describe below.

Perspective:
_____

Example:
_____

Counterargument:
_____

Third body paragraph: Did you address the issue with which you agree by presenting the argument, giving an example, stating why you agree, countering the argument, and refuting the argument? Yes or No (circle). Describe below.

Perspective:
_____

Example:
_____

Why you agree:

_____

Counterargument: _____

Refutation: _____

Conclusion: Did you reiterate your main points and end with a summary of your thesis? Yes or No (circle one)

Professional Tutoring ACT Essay Scoring Rubric

Grading Category	Yes?	Comments
Ideas and Analysis (12 points total)		
Precise, clear thesis		
Takes a position on the issue		
Evaluates all three perspectives		
Compares multiple perspectives		
Analyzes implications & underlying assumptions of perspectives		
Shows nuanced understanding of all 3 given perspectives		
Shows clear understanding of issue		
Ideas are relevant to the situation and to one another		
Analyzes relationship between the 3 perspectives		
Analysis is nuanced and insightful, not obvious or overly simplistic		
Perspectives are placed in context		
IDEAS & ANALYSIS SCORE		__/12
Development and Support (12 points total)		
Uses logical reasoning		
Ideas are clearly connected		
Arguments are not vague or repetitive		
Considers opposing viewpoints and objections		
Discussion of qualifications and complications of ideas		
Every claim made is supported by evidence or reasoning		
Gives at least 2 detailed examples		
Examples are relevant to issue and strengthen argument		
Evidence given is thoroughly explained		
DEVELOPMENT & SUPPORT SCORE		__/12
Organization (12 points total)		
5 paragraphs		
Clear introductory paragraph that states thesis		
3 body paragraphs with separate topics		
Clear conclusion		
Transitional sentences between each paragraph		
The examples follow the order in the introduction		
Transitions between ideas within paragraphs		

Ideas and evidence follow a logical sequence		
Essay is clearly unified by one main idea		
Each paragraph relates back to thesis		
Organizational structure enhances comprehension of argument		
ORGANIZATION SCORE		__/12
Language Use (12 points total)		
Uses present verb tense for literature		
Uses past tense for history		
Uses consistent verb tense for argument		
Uses parallelism		
Does not use contractions		
Does not use second person		
Appropriate tone and style		
Mostly active, minimal passive voice		
Varies sentence structure		
Uses correct spelling		
Uses punctuation correctly		
Subjects and verbs agree		
Nouns/Subject and pronouns agree		
Strong grasp of words' denotation/connotation		
Mature vocabulary		
Vocabulary does not "overwhelm" the essay		
Uses advanced techniques, e.g. "Rule of Three"		
Uses figurative language to strengthen argument		
Demonstrates proofreading		
LANGUAGE USE SCORE		__/12
Essay Grade (average of 4 category scores)		__/12
Additional Comments		

Sample Student Essays in response to published SAT & ACT prompts

The following essays are examples of responses to published SAT and ACT prompts, written by Professional Tutoring students. We, here at Professional Tutoring, have polished them up and modified them slightly, so that they better reflect what a "perfect" essay would look like.

Over the course of this class, you will take the SAT and ACT diagnostic tests that include the prompts that these essays are responding to. After you have completed your own essays, refer to these examples to see how you did to get ideas on how to improve.

"Redesigned" SAT Essays

1. Jimmy Carter: Foreword to *Arctic National Wildlife Refuge: Seasons of Life and Land: A Photographic Journey* by Subhankar Banerjee

2. Martin Luther King, Jr., "Beyond Vietnam – A Time to Break Silence". Excerpt of speech delivered in New York city on April 4, 1967

"Enhanced" ACT Essay

1. *"Free Music"*

2. *"Vocational Education"*

Re-Designed SAT Essay – Writing Sample – Exam #1: Jimmy Carter

In 2003, former President Jimmy Carter authored a foreword to a book featuring professional photographs of the Arctic National Wildlife Refuge. Carter was uniquely qualified to write this introduction to Subhankar Banerjee's book, as he had taken an instrumental role in preserving the 100 million acres of undisturbed land in the Arctic National Wildlife Refuge during his four-year presidency. Carter uses an amicable and awed tone to introduce this land that was so important to him and to gently, yet emotionally, encourage the protection of America's national heritage. Carter's thesis statement introduces his clear message, "The Arctic National Wildlife Refuge stands alone as America's last truly great wilderness." He encourages readers to conserve oil in daily life to protect this Arctic land. In the following essay, I will evaluate the impact that Carter's use of evidence, reasoning, and literary devices has on the effectiveness of his argument.

In this passage, Carter uses two types of evidence to support his arguments: personal experience and statistics. Through the majority of the passage, Carter relies on his personal experiences visiting the Refuge to share the beauty and, thus, the importance of protecting it. He shares with the reader the story of when he and his wife went camping there and saw the caribou. When describing the bipartisan support that the Arctic Refuge has, Carter uses specific statistics including the original 8.9-million-acre Refuge created by President Dwight D. Eisenhower, and his own signing of the Alaska National Interest Lands Conservation Act to "safeguard more than 100 million acres". In the seventh paragraph, Carter once again relies on statistics to strengthen his argument. He implores readers to use more efficient vehicles and debunks the idea that drilling in the Refuge would have any significant impact on oil production, citing the statistic that only 1-2 percent of the daily oil in the US could come from the Refuge. Although both types of evidence enhance his argument that the Arctic Refuge should be protected, his use of statistics gives us more concrete, logical, and convincing reasons.

President Carter employs the persuasive rhetorical techniques of pathos, ethos, and logos to convince his audience to protect the Arctic Refuge. In the first half of the passage, Carter mostly relies on emotional entreaties to persuade the reader. The implied reasoning is that if the reader realizes how beautiful the Arctic Refuge is, then they will not want to see that beauty destroyed. In the sixth paragraph, Carter again appeals to emotion, but with much stronger language. He evokes sympathy for the indigenous peoples who rely on the resources of this pristine land to live, even mentioning human rights. This type of reasoning could work on more sympathetic readers, but his argument would have been more persuasive if he had included more facts and purely logical arguments. In the fifth paragraph, Carter turns to ethos to represent his role as a United States president to establish his unique credibility to advocate for his land. As the second US president to oversee major legislation to increase and protect the Arctic Refuge, Carter is in a unique position to advocate for the protection of this land. He cites his building on President Eisenhower's earlier legislation to protest the destruction of this natural resource. This use of ethos is an effective way of gaining the reader's trust, because his role as a former president automatically affords him respect and it proves that he is knowledgeable about this topic. Even so, Carter's argument is at its most effective later on when he employs logos. He argues that the small amount of oil that could be obtained from the Refuge is not worth the environmental damage the drilling would cause, and uses the aforementioned statistical evidence to support his reasoning. He even offers up an alternative solution: driving more fuel-efficient cars.

Throughout the passage, Carter enhances his emotional arguments with the use of imagery. In the first three paragraphs, Carter depicts his passion for the Arctic National Wildlife Refuge. He talks about his visits, walking caribou trails, watching muskox, "shaggy survivors of the Ice Age" and brilliant mosaics of wildflowers. Carter sets up his later arguments for land protection with this soft use of imagery and appeal to emotion. His highly descriptive words prepare the reader to witness the photographs in the book. In the fourth paragraph Carter transitions from sharing his heartwarming experiences to using significantly stronger diction; the beauty of this "great wilderness" as described in the previous paragraphs is sharply juxtaposed with the "tragedy" of industrialization and his description of disturbing the "countless numbers of animals that depend on this northernmost ecosystem." The use of these literary devices reinforces his message and is intended to inspire the reader to share his desire of protecting the Arctic Refuge.

While Carter builds credibility with his presidential experience, his reliance on pathos and saccharine descriptions harm his arguments for environmental protection and undermine otherwise sound reasoning. His use of imagery does work well for the purpose of introducing photographs. However, the use of a photographic journal as a platform to protect one of the country's greatest national resources cannot possibly make much impact, locally, nationally or globally. Protecting the Arctic Refuge is a serious national issue. It seems that Carter would have little impact with this article.

<u>Re-Designed SAT Essay – Writing Sample – Exam #2: Martin Luther King, Jr.</u>

The Vietnam War was a gruesome war fought between the Viet Cong and the North Vietnamese Army versus the South Vietnamese Army and outside influences including the United States. The war was fought over the United States' containment policy; which was the containment of Communism to prevent the spread of communism (the Domino theory). Martin Luther King Jr. builds an argument to persuade his audience that involvement in the Vietnam War was unjust by suggesting a moral standpoint, relating the war to racial tensions in the United States, and spreading peaceful intentions.

The war in Vietnam, as suggested by Martin Luther King Jr., was morally wrong. King generates ethos by presenting his occupation, "Since I am a preacher by calling, I suppose it is not surprising that I have...major reasons for bringing Vietnam into the field of my moral vision" (1). King is credible of being a judge of ethical behavior because of his status in the church. King builds an argument by stating his status in the first line to persuade the audience to think like him because he is a moral leader. The first morally wrong point King brings up is the destruction of a poverty program, "Then came the build-up in Vietnam, and I watched this program [the poverty program] broken and eviscerated" (1). King further explains that he knew America would never invest in helping the poor as long as the resources of America were exhausted in the war.

Martin Luther King, Jr. also relates the war back to racial tensions in America. King juxtaposes the two countries: Vietnam and America. He compares the two showing that Blacks and Whites fight with and die for each other in Vietnam when the opposite is true in the United States: "we have been repeatedly faced with the cruel irony of watching Negro and White boys on TV screens as they kill and die together for a nation that has been unable to seat them together in the same schools" (1). King shows the irony in his juxtaposition to persuade the readers not only to support his Vietnam views but his Civil Rights Movement views. King generates pathos with his own experiences in the ghettos of the North. King witnessed many desperate, rejected, and angry young men who took to violent protests. In his experience, when King told them about non-violent protesting they would respond with, "What about Vietnam?" (2). King knew he could not denounce violence in the United States without addressing the world's violence. King uses this argument to persuade all the supporters of non-violence to stand with him against Vietnam.

King also tries to spread peace to his audience. King is faced with the exclusion of movements for peace because he is grouped together with the violent Civil Rights movements. However, King generates logos by explaining a conference he attended, "In 1957 when a group of us formed the Southern Christian Leadership Conference, we chose as our motto: 'To save the soul of America'" (2). He persuades his audience by disassociating himself from violent protest. King also persuades his audience by illustrating America's soul being poisoned, "If America's soul becomes totally poisoned, part of the autopsy must read: Vietnam" (2), persuading his audience even more that Vietnam is evil.

Martin Luther King Jr. builds an argument to persuade his audience that involvement in the Vietnam War is unjust by suggesting a moral standpoint, relating the war to racial tensions, and spreading peaceful intentions.

"Enhanced" ACT Essay – Writing Sample – Exam #3: *"Free Music"*

Music has changed both in style and accessibility throughout the years. Hundreds of years ago music was something that was only accessible to the wealthy with any frequency, but with the advancement of technology, music has become much more easily available than it used to be. Anyone can open up Spotify, Pandora, or YouTube and listen to all of the free music they want. Some think that this has lessened the value of music in some way, but I believe it has in fact led people to appreciate music more, and has helped more people discover new artists.

There are those who say that because music is so plentiful and either very cheap or free, it has lost value. This way of thinking implies that people appreciate music less because of the lower price and higher availability. I think this is incorrect. With more and more free music coming our way, people are more inclined to access it and listen to it. People listen to music in the car, when they are getting ready, at parties, at restaurants, or just alone in their homes. They are relating to more music, and will most likely continue to search for more relatable songs, often by new artists. More people listening to, discovering, and engaging with music in no way lessens its value. If anything, it increases it, because music has become such an indispensable part of so many people's lives.

Another perspective on music is that although we still value it, it is competing with other forms of entertainment for our attention. This insinuates that people would rather spend their time and money on these other types of entertainment. But these other forms of entertainment, such as movies, television, and video games, all use music in some way, even if it is only as a background. Jaws or Star Wars would seem totally different music without the soundtracks. Music is not competing with other forms of entertainment; it is enhancing them. Spending money on video games or movies does not mean we value music less.

In reality, having more music available has only increased appreciation for it. More people have the opportunity to discover new artists, and fall in love with new favorite bands. They can listen to more than just the same thirty songs repeating on the radio, without spending money not in their budget. This is a good thing, and it has increased many people's appreciation for music. Although some might argue that this lower price means music has lower value, economic value is not the same as cultural value. Free sources can only help the value of music to grow.

At the end of the day, music always has had and always will have value in our society. Lower prices and other forms of affordable entertainment have not changed this. Getting our music for free has only increased its value to our culture.

"Enhanced" ACT Essay – Writing Sample – Exam #3: "*Vocational Education*"

Vocational skills are skills that are needed when learning a trade and getting a job. Schools require certain academic courses, but there is a debate on whether vocational skill classes should also be provided at schools. Although some do believe that career-training classes are helpful to those who do not excel academically, vocational skill classes should not be offered at public schools.

The belief that career classes will help some students who are not successful in academic classes is valid, however academic classes will help in all fields of jobs and are good, and often necessary, to have as background knowledge. In contrast, career classes focus on only one thing or skill, which does not help students broaden their horizons to find new interests, and will not serve them well if they ever change their choice of career. Additionally, students should be pushed to do better in their academic classes instead of encouraged to replace them with specific vocational training. Even if they do end up in the exact careers they trained for, they will probably need the skills their academic classes were trying to teach them.

Another point of view is that skilled workers require knowledge and advanced communication skills, which are learned in academic classes. This belief is accurate and reasonable. Every job requires these types of skills, and academic courses are what teach them to students most effectively, thus preparing them for all possible careers. For example, English classes teach students how to read critically and how to write: two skills that are needed for almost every job out there. Most jobs require a person to use at least some basic math skills, and understanding current events requires a basic understanding of history and government. Vocational classes are not designed to teach students these fundamental skills, and are too narrowly focused to do this properly. The skills learned in vocational classes cannot replace the knowledge that needs to be acquired through academics.

One last argument for schools to focus on academics instead of vocational training is that no one knows what jobs will look like or require in the future. For example, there may not be a need for someone to carve wood to make a bench if a machine can be used to achieve the same level of quality. In addition, many jobs will come about that do not exist right now. Training a student in a particular area will not be beneficial because the job may not be necessary in the future, which wastes both the student's time and as well as the school's budget. Career-based courses are more expensive than academic courses because they are more hands on and require more resources and equipment. That money could be better spent providing more resources for core academic classes.

In conclusion, career classes that provide vocational skills are not beneficial to a school or its students and will only be a waste of time and money. Although the classes give a student further insight into a job, they will not help if the student does not choose that job as their career or if that job is not needed in the future. As technology advances, fewer jobs are needed to do certain tasks; therefore, a student should not look into the specifics of a technical profession until college. Academic courses offer a broad enough curriculum to allow students to explore different interests, and give them enough background knowledge to prepare them for whatever their future will look like.

BARNHART

McDougal, Littell
English Gold Level

McDougal, Littell
English Red Level

INSIGHT: The Experience of Literature

ENGLISH WORKSHOP

WEBSTER'S NINTH NEW COLLEGIATE DICTIONARY

THE FACTS ON FILE ENCYCLOPEDIA OF WORD AND PHRASE ORIGINS   HENDRICKSON

STEVENSON   WORDS   VAN NOSTRAND REINHOLD

McCrum, Cran, and MacNeil   THE STORY OF ENGLISH

THE VIKING LIBRARY

THE NEW BOOK OF KNOWLEDGE

Chapter 4

Vocabulary Exercises

In this chapter:
• SAT Vocabulary Exercise Instructions
• SAT Vocabulary Exercises 1 - 15

SAT Vocabulary Exercise Instructions

Vocabulary study and improvement is vital for the Critical Reading and Writing sections of the SAT Exam. It is also the most boring and tedious part of SAT/ACT Preparation. I always think of studying vocabulary like doing sit ups. Sit-ups are boring and somewhat painful, but they do pay off in core strengthening. Vocabulary review will strengthen your core SAT/ACT knowledge.

The SAT has been re-designed to be more like the ACT, and now focuses on "high-utility academic words and phrases," or "Tier Two" vocabulary. These Tier Two words appear in many different texts across different domains, and they often have multiple meanings, which makes understanding the context in which they are used even more important. Included in this text are 15 vocabulary lists that include the *365 Most Frequent SAT Vocabulary Words*.

For each Vocabulary Unit, complete the "definitions" page by writing the definition in the space provided. Make sure to take note of words that have multiple or alternate meanings. Use your choice of traditional or online dictionary.

Unit 1 SAT Vocabulary

1. aberration _____

2. aloof _____

3. astray _____

4. brevity _____

5. compliment _____

6. corroborate _____

7. desolate _____

8. distinguish _____

9. engage _____

10. explicit _____

11. futile _____

12. hybrid _____

13. incline _____

14. interpretation _____

15. lethargic _____

16. meekness _____

17. noble _____

18. parenthetical _____

19. poles _____

20. proficient _____

21. rash _____

22. reserve _____

23. sequester _____

24.. subservient _____

25. testament _____

Unit 2 SAT Vocabulary

1. abolish _____

2. altercation _____

3. atrophy _____

4. broach _____

5. compose _____

6. credence _____

7. despoil _____

8. diverge _____

9. engender _____

10. exploit _____

11. galvanize _____

12. hyperbole _____

13. incontestable _____

14. interval _____

15. liable _____

16. melancholy _____

17. nostalgia _____

18. passively _____

19. portrayal _____

20. profound _____

21. rational _____

22. residual _____

23. shards _____

24. substantiate _____

25. transient _____

Unit 3 SAT Vocabulary

1. abridge _____

2. amass _____

3. attribute _____

4. burgeon _____

5. concede _____

6. crude _____

7. detach _____

8. dreary _____

9. engross _____

10. exponent _____

11. gauge _____

12. idolize _____

13. incredulous _____

14. intricate _____

15. lineage _____

16. menacing _____

17. notion _____

18. pathogen _____

19. postulate _____

20. project _____

21. realm _____

22. resignation _____

23. simulations _____

24. subversion _____

25. treacherous _____

Unit 4 SAT Vocabulary

1. abstract _____

2. ambiguous _____

3. augment _____

4. cache _____

5. conceivable _____

6. culminate _____

7. detriment _____

8. drench _____

9. engulf _____

10. exquisite _____

11. generalize _____

12. ignominy _____

13. increments _____

14. inverse _____

15. listless _____

16. mercurial _____

17. novel _____

18. patrons _____

19. potent _____

20. prolong _____

21. reap _____

22. resolute _____

23. sinister _____

24. succinct _____

25. undermines _____

Unit 5 SAT Vocabulary

1. accolade _____

2. ambivalence _____

3. austere _____

4. candid _____

5. condescend _____

6. cultivate _____

7. deviate _____

8. dubious _____

9. enigmatic _____

10. facets _____

11. genre _____

12. illusion _____

13. indifference _____

14. invocation _____

15. long _____

16. meticulous _____

17. objective _____

18. penchant _____

19. practicality _____

20. prominent _____

21. recalcitrant _____

22. respite _____

23. skeptical _____

24. suffrage _____

25. underpins _____

Unit 6 SAT Vocabulary

1. accommodate _____

2. anecdote _____

3. authenticate _____

4. capitulate _____

5. conductivity _____

6. cumbersome _____

7. devise _____

8. earnest _____

9. entail _____

10. facilitate _____

11. germane _____

12. imminent _____

13. indigenous _____

14. invoke _____

15. lucid _____

16. metropolis _____

17. obliterate _____

18. pensive _____

19. pragmatic _____

20. prone _____

21. recant _____

22. retrospect _____

23. solemn _____

24. sullen _____

25. underscore _____

Unit 7 SAT Vocabulary

1. acquiesce _____

2. anomalous _____

3. autocrat _____

4. capricious _____

5. confer _____

6. curator _____

7. devoid _____

8. eccentric _____

9. entity _____

10. fastidious _____

11. glut _____

12. immure _____

13. indignation _____

14. irksome _____

15. lucrative _____

16. mishap _____

17. obscure _____

18. perceives _____

19. precede _____

20. proprietor _____

21. reciprocal _____

22. revamp _____

23. solicitude _____

24. summon _____

25. undetectable _____

Unit 8 SAT Vocabulary

1. acquisition _____

2. antagonistic _____

3. baffle _____

4. catalyst _____

5. congenial _____

6. cursory _____

7. devour _____

8. eclipse _____

9. enumerate _____

10. feasible _____

11. grandeur _____

12. impartial _____

13. indulge _____

14. irrefutable _____

15. lurching _____

16. mitigate _____

17. obsolete _____

18. peril _____

19. precipitation _____

20. prospective _____

21. refute _____

22. reverberate _____

23. somber _____

24. superficially _____

25. undulating _____

Unit 9 SAT Vocabulary

1. adhere _____

2. antipathy _____

3. bare _____

4. cease _____

5. conjure _____

6. cynic _____

7. diffuse _____

8. edict _____

9. ephemeral _____

10. feign _____

11. grandiose _____

12. imperative _____

13. industrious _____

14. jargon _____

15. magnanimous _____

16. mode _____

17. obstinacy _____

18. perpetual _____

19. precipitous _____

20. prosperous _____

21. relentless _____

22. reverence _____

23. sovereign _____

24. surge _____

25. unfounded _____

Unit 10 SAT Vocabulary

1. admonish _____

2. apathy _____

3. barren _____

4. celestial _____

5. consecrate _____

6. daunt _____

7. digress _____

8. eloquent _____

9. epitome _____

10. ferocity _____

11. gratify _____

12. imperceptible _____

13. inevitable _____

14. judicious _____

15. malicious _____

16. modest _____

17. obstruct _____

18. persecuted _____

19. precise _____

20. protagonists _____

21. relevant _____

22. revive _____

23. sparse _____

24. surreptitious _____

25. unprecedented _____

Unit 11 SAT Vocabulary

1. adversarial

2. appall

3. befall

4. censure

5. consensus

6. debilitate

7. diligence

8. embellish

9. erratic

10. fidelity

11. hail

12. impertinent

13. inexorable

14. jurisdiction

15. malignant

16. molding

17. odyssey

18. pervasive

19. predecessors

20. provocative

21. relish

22. rhetoric

23. spawning

24. susceptible

25. unseemly

Unit 12 SAT Vocabulary

1. adverse _____

2. apprehension _____

3. belittle _____

4. chagrin _____

5. constitute _____

6. defer _____

7. diminish _____

8. embody _____

9. esthetic _____

10. fiscal _____

11. hardship _____

12. impervious _____

13. infer _____

14. juxtapose _____

15. malleable _____

16. momentous _____

17. omniscient _____

18. phenomenon _____

19. predominant _____

20. proximity _____

21. render _____

22. rudimentary _____

23. speculate _____

24. sustainable _____

25. urbane _____

Unit 13 SAT Vocabulary

1. advocate _____

2. arcane _____

3. belligerent _____

4. cloister _____

5. construe _____

6. degrade _____

7. discord _____

8. eminent _____

9. ethereal _____

10. flank _____

11. hasten _____

12. implicit _____

13. infrastructure _____

14. kin _____

15. marginal _____

16. monotony _____

17. onerous _____

18. pinnacle _____

19. preoccupation _____

20. proxy _____

21. replenish _____

22. satiate _____

23. squalid _____

24. symbolic _____

25. usurp _____

Unit 14 SAT Vocabulary

1. affiliate _____

2. aristocratic _____

3. benefactor _____

4. coalesce _____

5. consummate _____

6. delusion _____

7. discrepant _____

8. empirical _____

9. evoke _____

10. fleet _____

11. hiatus _____

12. imply _____

13. ingenious _____

14. laborious _____

15. maternal _____

16. morbid _____

17. onset _____

18. pioneering _____

19. preposterous _____

20. prudent _____

21. replete _____

22. satire _____

23. stark _____

24. synthetic _____

25. utmost _____

Unit 15 SAT Vocabulary

1. affirm _____

2. arouse _____

3. benevolent _____

4. coherent _____

5. contingent _____

6. demean _____

7. disdain _____

8. emulate _____

9. evolve _____

10. flourish _____

11. hinder _____

12. impose _____

13. inherent _____

14. labyrinthine _____

15. mature _____

16. mundane _____

17. oppression _____

18. pious _____

19. prescribed _____

20. pungent _____

21. replicate _____

22. scorn _____

23. static _____

24. tact _____

25. vantage _____

Unit 16 SAT Vocabulary

1. aggregate _____

2. array _____

3. benign _____

4. colloquial _____

5. continuum _____

6. demographic _____

7. dismay _____

8. enclave _____

9. exacerbate _____

10. foreseeable _____

11. homage _____

12. impudent _____

13. inquire _____

14. laden _____

15. maxim _____

16. municipal _____

17. ornate _____

18. pity _____

19. presided _____

20. qualitative _____

21. repose _____

22. scrutinize _____

23. stellar _____

24. tangent _____

25. veer _____

Unit 17 SAT Vocabulary

1. agitate

2. articulate

3. bequeath

4. combative

5. convene

6. depict

7. disparage

8. encroach

9. exclusion

10. franchise

11. hone

12. inadvertent

13. insatiable

14. lament

15. means

16. naïve

17. ostentatious

18. plausible

19. presumption

20. quasi

21. repressed

22. secluded

23. stratosphere

24. tangible

25. venerable

Unit 18 SAT Vocabulary

1. allegory _____

2. ascertain _____

3. besiege _____

4. commodity _____

5. conventional _____

6. deplete _____

7. disparate _____

8. endow _____

9. exemplify _____

10. frank _____

11. humane _____

12. inalienable _____   _____

13. insolent _____

14. latent _____

15. measured _____

16. nefarious _____

17. overt _____

18. plight _____

19. prevailing _____

20. querulous _____

21. repudiates _____

22. seek _____

23. subjugate _____

24. tedious _____

25. venture _____

Unit 19 SAT Vocabulary

1. alleviate _____

2. assert _____

3. bias _____

4. compensate _____

5. converge _____

6. deposit _____

7. dispense _____

8. endure _____

9. exert _____

10. fraudulent _____

11. humble _____

12. incendiary _____

13. intact _____

14. latitudes _____

15. mediation _____

16. negligible _____

17. panacea _____

18. plumes _____

19. principle _____

20. quirk _____

21. rescind _____

22. sensory _____

23. subordinate _____

24. tenuous _____

25. veritable _____

Unit 20 SAT Vocabulary

1. allude _____

2. assess _____

3. blatant _____

4. compile _____

5. correlate _____

6. derision _____

7. disposition _____

8. enfranchise _____

9. expedite _____

10. fuse _____

11. hurtle _____

12. incite _____

13. integrate _____

14. laud _____

15. medium _____

16. nexus _____

17. paradox _____

18. poignant _____

19. pristine _____

20. ramified _____

21. reservations _____

22. sentinels _____

23. subsequently _____

24. terrestrial _____

25. viable _____

Unit 21 SAT Vocabulary

1. virtually   _____

2. volition   _____

3. waned   _____

4. wary   _____

5. wily   _____

6. wont   _____

7. yearning   _____

8. yield   _____

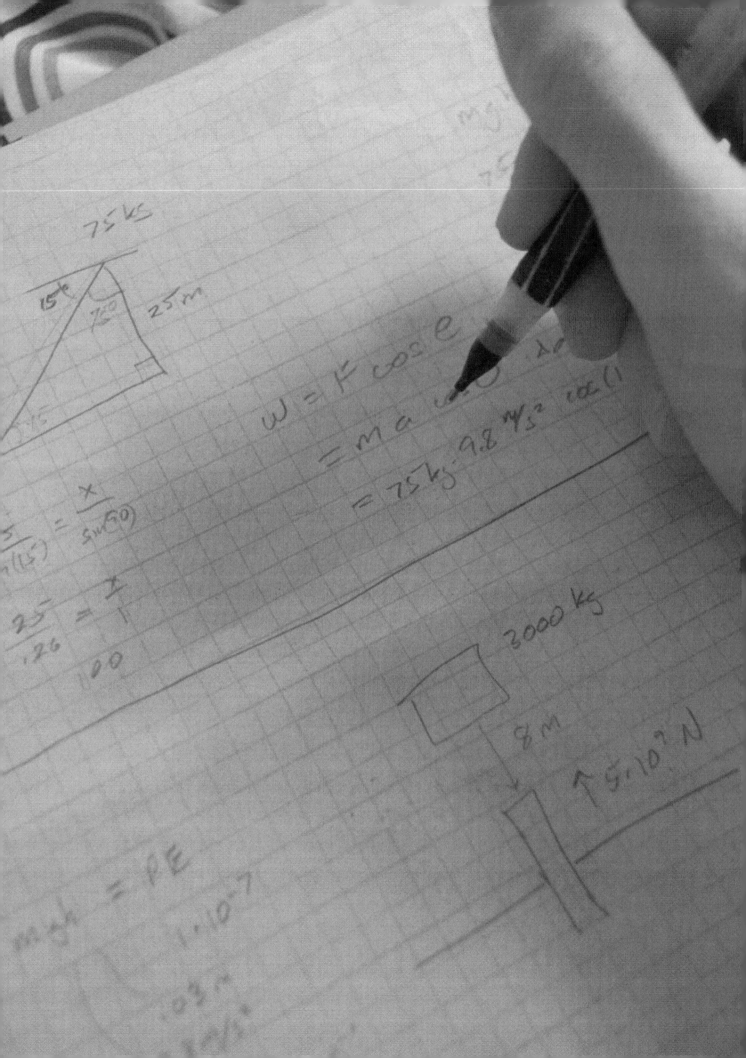

75 kg

15° 75° 25m

$\frac{s}{n(15°)} = \frac{x}{\sin(50)}$

$\frac{25}{.26} = \frac{x}{100}$

$W = F \cos \theta$

$= m a \cos \theta$

$= 75 kg \cdot 9.8 \, m/s^2 \cos(1$

3000 kg

8 m

$5 \cdot 10^2 N$

$= PE$

$1 \cdot 10^{-7}$

Chapter 5

Math: Algebra & Geometry

In this chapter:

- Math Overview

- Algebra

- Geometry

Math Overview

Math is one of the two subscores on the SAT, and one of four subscores on the ACT. The majority of the math portions of the SAT and ACT will focus on Algebra I and II. While a calculator is not strictly required to succeed on these exams, most students prefer to have one. One note to remember is that QWERTY format calculators are not permitted.

The SAT Math test is scored on a scale of 200-800 points. This test has two different sections: one 25-minute section with a calculator and one 55-minute section with a calculator. The ACT Math section is scored from 1-36, and has one 60-minute math section. Topics covered on these tests include high school Algebra I and II, Geometry, numbers and operations, statistics, probability, and trigonometry. The majority of the questions on the SAT are multiple choice, although both the calculator and no-calculator sections include free response questions at the end, which students will handwrite into a grid-in format. All of the questions on the ACT are multiple choice. Math questions are arranged in a "ladder of difficulty," with questions becoming progressively more difficult.

Students will earn one point for each correct answer. No points are deducted for wrong answers.

Strategies

The strategy for the math section is similar to the one you have already reviewed in the Reading and Writing Sections. Unlike the Reading and Writing Sections, the Math Section will require that you are very careful in working out each step of your numerical exercises. The SAT and ACT know where students commit the most errors and will take advantage of your mistakes. These are some basic strategies to keep in mind:

1. If you do not know how to begin a problem, just start with what you do know. One rule of thumb is to factor first, if possible.

2. If the problem is esoteric (weird, incomprehensible) with no numbers and only variables, plug in numbers that work for you so that you can develop some direction.

3. Remember that an answer must ALWAYS work (unless specified otherwise).

4. When you are testing answer choices, remember to stay away from numbers that function as identities, e.g., 1 and 2. And, always check 0.

5. If a problem is taking more than three to four steps, you are probably missing an easy shortcut. See your SAT prep course instructor for any problems like this.

Algebra

The following algebra review is divided into 15 units of study. The topics progress from basic arithmetic to logic and also include word problem review units.

Since the problems can be used for further review, write neatly and SHOW your work. Answers for each problem are provided in Chapter 6.

Unit 1: Basic Arithmetic

Define:

Sum: _____

Difference: _____

Product: _____

Quotient: _____

Factors: _____

Digit: _____

Integers: _____

Whole Numbers: _____

Solve:

1)
```
    963
    368
    741
    147
  + 148
```

2)
```
    987
    654
    321
    456
  + 789
```

3)
```
   9874
   6541
   3210
   1235
 + 4567
```

4)
```
   6555
   5444
   4333
   3222
 + 2580
```

5)
```
   1574
   1982
    532
   8111
 + 6789
```

6)
```
   5877
   9565
   3232
   4512
 + 4893
```

7)
```
   1808
  - 888
```

8)
```
    384
  -  99
```

9)
```
    703
  - 289
```

10) $575 * 936 =$

11) $7117 * 797 =$

12)   4334 and 427 are factors of what product?

13)   Find the product of 725 and 305.

14)   What is 528 multiplied by 962?

15) $98,765 \div 39 =$

16) $4914 \div 39 =$

17)   Find the quotient of 1024 and 16.

18)   Divide 0 by 7432.

19)   Divide 7432 by 0.

Order of Operations

PEMDAS stands for: _____

_____

Solve:

20) $5(27 + 6) + 5(-7 - 4) =$

21) $4 * 6 - 11 + 6 \div 3 =$

22) $46 - (21 - 7 - 3) =$

23) $9(8 - 5)^3 =$

24) $5(5 - 0)(5 - 5)(4 - 3) =$

25)   Find the value of $14 + 5 * 3 - 3^2$

26)   Change two operation signs so that the value of the expression in the question above is 8.

Algebra Unit 2: Polynomials

Define:

Variable: _____

Monomial: _____

Binomial: _____

Trinomial: _____

Numerical
coefficient: _____

Base: _____

Exponent: _____

Notes:

1. Make sure that variables match so that you can add or subtract the polynomials.
    e.g.: $x^3 + 2x^2 \neq 3x^5$

2. Be sure to distribute negative signs.
    e.g.: $(2x^2 - 2x - 5) - (x^2 + 8x - 12) =$
    $2x^2 - 2x - 5 - x^2 - 8x + 12 = x^2 - 10x + 7$

3. Standard form of a polynomial means that the degree of its monomial terms decreases from left to right.

Addition and Subtraction of Polynomials

1) $-3y + 12 + y^2 + 3y + 12$

2) $3(x^2 + 2xy + y^2) - 2(x^2 - y^2) + x^2 - 2xy + y^2$

3) $-4x^3 - 2x^2 + x - 5 + 2x^3 + 3x + 4$

4) $(x^3y - 2xy^2 + 3xy) - (4xy^2 - 3x^2y + 2xy)$

5) $10x - 2\big(3x - (x - 2) + 3(x + 3)\big)$

6) $2x^2 - x + 3 + 3x^2 - 4x + 7$

7) $(p^4 - 2p^3 - 3p^2 + 7p + 1) + 2(p^3 - 3p^2 - 4p + 6)$

8) $6x^2 + 5 + 3 - 2x^2$

9) $-3(x^2 - 5x) - 2(3x - 2x^2 + 5)$

10) $y^2 + 3y^4 - (y^5 - y^4)$

Multiplication and Division of Polynomials

11) $(x + 1)(x + 5)$

12) $(3x + 1)(2x + 2)$

13) $(x - 3)(3x + 1)$

14) $(x^2 + 9)(x^2 - x - 4)$

15) $(2x - 5)(x + 6)$

16) $(3x^2 + x - 5)(2x^2 - 5x + 4)$

17) $(x + \frac{1}{4})(x - \frac{1}{2})$

18) $(x^2 + 4x - 9)(x^2 - \frac{1}{2})$

19) $3a(5a + 4)$

20) $-2x^2(3x^3 - 2x^2 - 4x + 3)$

21) $3x^2yz^3(2xy - yz + 5x^2z^2)$

22) $(x^3 y^4 z^5)(3x^8 yz^3)$

23) $81x^6 y^5 / 27x^3 y$

24) $-144a^3 b^2 c^5 / 30ac^4$

25)   Divide $4x^2 y^3$ into $(-12x^5 y^8 + 8x^3 y^6)$

26) $(54a^7 b^2 - 27a^6 b^5)/3a^3 b^3$

27) $(18x^2y^3 - 48x^4y^2 + 27x^3y^4)/-3xy^2$

28) $(36a^3b^4 - 24a^4b^3 + 8a^2b^2)/2ab^2$

29) $\dfrac{.3(6)}{.6}$

30) $(15p^2q^2 - 5pq^3 + 10p)/5pq$

31)   A nutritionist studied the U.S. consumption of carrots and celery and of broccoli over a 6-yr period. The nutritionist modeled the results, in millions of pounds, with the following polynomials.

Carrots and celery: $-12x^3 + 106x^2 - 241x + 4477$

Broccoli: $14x^2 - 14x + 1545$

In each polynomial, $x = 0$ corresponds to the first year in the 6-yr period. What polynomial models the total number of pounds, in millions, of carrots, celery, and broccoli consumed in the United States during the 6-yr period?

32)   The number of students at East High School and the number of students at Central High School over a 10-year period can be modeled by the following polynomials.

East High School: $-11x^2 + 133x + 1200$

Central High School: $-7x^2 + 95x + 1100$

In each polynomial, $x = 0$ corresponds to the first year in the 10-year period. What polynomial models the total number of students at both high schools?

Algebra Unit 3: Exponents

Notes:

1. **Basic Rules:**

   $a^0 = 1$ any number $^0 = 1$

   $a^1 = a$ any number $^1 = $ itself

   $a^2 = a * a$ $a^3 = a * a * a$ (and so on)

2. **Addition/**

   Subtraction: Both bases and exponents must match!

3. **Multiplication:**   Same bases, add the exponents

   $a^2 * a^5 = a^{2+5} = a^7$

   Different bases, list alphabetically by variable

   $a^2 * b^5 = a^2 b^5$

4. **Division:**   As shown in last unit, subtract exponents when bases match.

   $81x^6 y^5 / 27x^3 y = 3x^3 y^4$

5. **Raising to a power:**   Multiply exponents

   $(a^2)^3 = a^{2 \times 3} = a^6$

6. **Negative Exponents:**   Negative exponents cause their corresponding base (number or variable) to change location from the numerator to the denominator or from the denominator to the numerator.

   $\frac{1}{a^{-5}} = \frac{a^5}{1}$ and $\frac{a^{-5}}{1} = \frac{1}{a^5}$

7. **Quotient of Powers:** $\left(\frac{a}{b}\right)^n = \frac{a^n}{b^n}$

8. **Negative Signs:**   Be careful of negative signs:

   $(-a)^2 = a^2$ the negative sign is in ( )

   $-a^2 = -a^2$ the negative sign is NOT in ( )

   $-(a)^2 = -a^2$ the negative sign is NOT in ( )

9. **Order of Operations:**   Always follow PEMDAS!

Positive Exponents

1) $(-9)^2$

2) $2x^2 = 32$

3) $(5^5)^4$

4) $(\frac{1}{2}x^6)^2$

5) $(3*7)^4$

6) $(16*2)^2$

7) $((-3xy)^2)^3$

8) $(9a^3)^2 * (2a)^3$

9) $(-ab)(a^2b)^2$

10) $(-x)^5(-x)^2(-x)^3$

11) $(-3xy^2)^3 * (-2x^2y)^2$

12) $4^2 * 4^4$

13) $2^x = 4$

What is 2^{2x}?

14) $2^4 = 4^x$

What is x?

15) $128^{\frac{1}{2}} = 16^x$

What is x?

Negative Exponents

16) x^{-9}

17) $5x^{-4}$

18) $3a^{-2}$

19) $(15x)^{-2}$

20) $(\frac{1}{4}x)^{-5}$

21) $a^{-2}y^3$

22) $3a^{-3}b^{-8}$

23) $6a^{-2}b^{-4}$

24) $1/(7a^{-4}b^{-1})$

25) $(81a^{-6}b^5)/(27a^9b^7)$

26) $(-144a^3b^2c^5)/(30a^{-5}c^8)$

27) $(54a^{-7}b^2 - 27a^6b^{-5})/(3a^3b^{-3})$

28) $\dfrac{18a^2b^3 - 48a^{-4}b^{-2} + 27a^3b^4}{-3ab^{-2}}$

29) $(6a^{-3}b^4 - 24a^4b^{-6} + 8a^2b^2)/(2a^{-1}b^2)$

30) $(-12a^{-5} + 8a^{-8}b^{-2})/(4a^{-3}b^{-2})$

31) $\dfrac{6x}{18y^{-2}} * \dfrac{y^3x^{-5}}{x^3}$

32) $\dfrac{-3x^5}{x^{13}} * \dfrac{2x^{10}y}{15y^3}$

33) $\dfrac{y^{10}}{2x^3} * \dfrac{20x^{14}}{xy^3}$

34) $\dfrac{5x^{-5}}{x^{13}} * \dfrac{2x^{10}y^6}{10y^7}$

Solve for the variable

35) $4^x * 4^2 = 4^5$

36) $\dfrac{x^2}{x^a} = x^5$

37) $a^{-1} = \dfrac{1}{6}$

38) $\dfrac{b^6}{6b^{-4}} * \dfrac{12}{10b^7} = 36$

Word Problems

39) The power generated by a wind turbine depends on wind speed. The expression $800v^3$ gives the power in watts for a certain wind turbine at wind speed v in meters per second. If the wind speed triples, by what factor does the power (in watts) generated by the wind turbine increase?

40)   Rewrite the expression $49x^2y^2z^2$ using only one exponent.

41)   The hull speed, s, in nautical miles per hour of a sailboat can be modeled by the formula $s = 1.34\sqrt{l}$, where l is the length in feet of the sailboat's waterline.

Find the speed of a boat whose hull length is 10 feet. Round your answer to the nearest tenth of a nautical mile.

42)   The radius of a cylinder is 7.8×10m. The height of the cylinder is 3.4×10^{-2}m. What is the volume of the cylinder? Write your answer in scientific notation. (hint: $V = \pi r^2 h$)

43)   A snail travels at a speed of 3×10^{-2}mi/h. What is the snail's speed in inches per minute?

Algebra Unit 4: Radicals and Square Roots

Perfect Squares

a) 1^2

b) 2^2

c) 3^2

d) 4^2

e) 5^2

f) 6^2

g) 7^2

h) 8^2

i) 9^2

j) 10^2

k) 11^2

l) 12^2

m) 13^2

n) 14^2

o) 15^2

p) 16^2

q) 17^2

r) 18^2

s) 19^2

t) 20^2

u) 21^2

v) 22^2

w) 23^2

x) 24^2

y) 25^2

Notes:

1) Radicals are similar to variables. Only matching radicals may be added together. Non-matching and matching variables may be multiplied.

2) Radicals may be written with the radical ($\sqrt{}$) sign or with exponents. e.g.: $x^{1/2} = \sqrt{x}$. $x^{2/3} = \sqrt[3]{x^2}$.

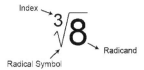

3) The index of a radical expression must always be a positive integer greater than **1**. When no index is written it is assumed to be **2**, or a square root.

4) Even indices yield both a positive and negative root. Odd indices yield only one root which matches the sign of the radicand.

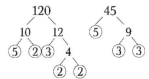

5) Make factor trees.   Circle all prime numbers.

6) When a radicand in a denominator is not a perfect square, you may need to rationalize the denominator to remove the radical. Multiply the numerator by the same radical expression. Choose an expression that makes the radicand in the denominator a perfect square.

7) Be aware of the quadratic formula which will be used in Unit 5: $x = \dfrac{-b \pm \sqrt{b^2 - 4ac}}{2a}$

Practice Problems – Radicals

1) $\sqrt{40}$ 2) $\sqrt{75}$ 3) $(162)^{1/3}$

4) $\sqrt{.0121}$

5) $\sqrt{0.16}$

6) $(294y^2)^{1/2}$

7) $125^{1/3}$

8) $-32,768^{1/3}$

9) $10241^{1/10}$

10) $16^{-3/2}$

11) $8^{-2/3}$

12) $1000^{3/2}$

13) $\sqrt[3]{27xy^3}$

14) $\sqrt[6]{32x * 2}$

15) $(6^{\frac{2}{3}} * 6^{\frac{1}{4}})^{\frac{12}{11}}$

16) $\frac{1}{2}\sqrt{80}$

17) $2\sqrt{5/4}$

18) $\sqrt{112}/\sqrt{175}$

19) $5^{1/2} * 15^{1/2}$

20) $\sqrt{10} * \sqrt{20}$

21) $\sqrt{2} * \sqrt{6} * \sqrt{3}$

22) $(\frac{2}{3} * \sqrt{3})^2$

23) $(\frac{1}{2} * \sqrt{8})^{1/2}$

24) $(2\sqrt{5})/\sqrt{4}$

Practice Problems – Radical Equations

25) $\sqrt{x} = 15$

26) $\sqrt{(x + 25)} = 25$

27) $\sqrt[4]{(b + 12)} = 6$

28) $\sqrt{3x + 1} = \sqrt{x + 9}$

29) $\sqrt{3x + 6} + \sqrt{6x + 4} = 0$

30) $\sqrt{b + 12} = b + 6$

31) $\sqrt[5]{5x + 6} + \sqrt[5]{7x - 4} = 0$

32) $\sqrt{7x + 4} - 6x - 4 = 0$

33) $\sqrt{3x + 7} = x + 6$

34) $\sqrt[3]{5x + 6} = (7x - 4)^{2/3}$

Radical Equation Word Problems

35) You throw a ball upward. Its height h, in feet, after t seconds can be modeled by the function $h = -16t^2 + 30t + 6$. After how many seconds will it hit the ground?

36)   Juan and Lenore met for lunch. At 1 p.m., they parted ways. Maybe forever, considering how they left things. Juan drove due south at 30 mph and Lenore drove due east at 60 mph. Apparently, she was more upset than he was. At 1:30 p.m., how far away are Juan and Lenore from each other?

37)   The distance, d, in miles that a person can see to the horizon can be modeled by the formula $d = \sqrt{\frac{3h}{2}}$ where h is the person's height above sea level in feet. To the nearest tenth of a mile, how far to the horizon can a person see if they are 100 feet above sea level? Round your answer to the nearest tenth of a mile.

38)   Find the area of a rectangle with a length of $5 + 2\sqrt{5}$ and a width of $3 + 7\sqrt{5}$

39)   The voltage of an iPhone speaker is $V = 4\sqrt{P}$, where P is the power of the speaker. What is the voltage of a 400-watt speaker?

Algebra Unit 5: Factoring

Notes:

1.   Factoring is the opposite of foiling.

2.   Make sure to take out the greatest common factor first.

3.   Factoring patterns are always the same!
   Difference of two squares: $x^2 - y^2 = (x - y)(x + y)$
   Sum of two squares: Not possible w/o imaginary numbers
   Sum of two cubes: $x^3 + y^3 = (x + y)(x^2 - xy + y^2)$
   Difference of two cubes: $x^3 - y^3 = (x - y)(x^2 + xy + y^2)$

4.   Grouping:
   Pull out the common factors, first, and then group the parentheses.
   1) Make sure that exponents are in descending order. Re-write, if necessary.
   2) Put parentheses around the 1st and 2nd terms and the 3rd and 4th terms.
   3) Pull out the common factors(s).
   4) Write the factors (in parentheses) that occur twice.
   5) Write the other two factors and the sign between them.
      e.g.: $x^3 + 2x^2 + 3x + 6 = x^2(x + 2) + 3(x + 2) = (x^2 + 3)(x + 2)$

5.   Real Number Solutions of Quadratics are based on the equation's discriminant: $\sqrt{b^2 - 4ac}$
   Discriminant $= 0$: One real solution
   Discriminant > 0: Two real solutions
   Discriminant < 0: No real solutions

Find the Greatest Common Factor (GCF)

1) $7x^3,\ 28x,\ 14x^4$ 2) $16a^2b,\ 84ab^2,\ 36a^2b^2$

3) $10ab^2,\ 25a^3b^2,\ 80a^2b$

Factor the GCF

4) $2x^2 - 4$

5) $4a - 12$

6) $4p^2q^3 + 24p^3q - 16p^3q^2$

7) $-7xy^2z^4 + 21x^2y^3z^2 - 84x^3z^2$

8) $x(x - 3) + 5(x - 3)$

9) $p(p^2 - 1) + 4(p^2 - 1)$

Difference of Two Squares

10) $x^2 - 36$

11) $y^2 - 81$

12) $49 - x^2$

13) $(x - y)^2 - 81$

14) $75z^2 - 147b^2$

15) $(2x + 3)^2 - 64$

Trinomials

16) $x^2 - 8x + 15$

17) $y^2 + 3y - 4$

18) $x^2 + 32 + 12x$

19) $y^2 + 13y + 22$

20) $48 - 16x + x^2$

21) $y^2 + 3y - 18$

Solving for a Variable

22) $(x + 1)(x + 2) = 0$

23) $y^2 + 5y - 6 = 0$

24) $2y^2 + 5y + 3 = 0$

25) $3x(4x^2 - 1) = 0$

26) $y^2 + 32y + 256 = 0$

27) $9x^2 - 81 = 0$

Sums and Differences of Cubes

28) $x^3 - 8$

29) $x^3 + 64$

30) $400x^3 - 50$

31) $32x^3 - 4$

32) $3x^3 + 81$

33) $40x^3 - 5$

Grouping

34) $30x^3 + 40x^2 + 3x + 4$

35) $9x^3 + 18x^2 + 7x + 14$

36) $18x^3 + 30x^2 + 3x + 5$

37) $5x^3 - 20x^2 + 3x - 12$

38) $18x^3 - 2x^2 + 27x - 3$

39) $-2x^3 - 4x^2 - 3x - 6$

Evaluate the Discriminant and Number of Solutions

40) $2x^2 + 7x - 15 = 0$

41) $6x^2 = 2x + 7$

42) $17x^2 = 12x - 3$

43) $8x(x + 6) = 0$

44) $-4x^2 + 12x - 16 = 0$ 45) $5x^2 + 20x = -25$

1)   If $\frac{1}{y} = \sqrt{36}$, then $y =$

2) $4\sqrt{96} - 3\sqrt{216}$

3) $(.4x^3)^2 =$

4) $\sqrt{\frac{x^2}{4} + \frac{4x^2}{9}} =$

5) $x + y = 7$ and $x^2 - y^2 = 56$, then $x - y =$

6) $x^2 - y^2 = 121$ and $x + y = 11$, then $x - y =$

7)   If $20x - 20y = 40$, what is: $4x - 4y =$

8) $2\sqrt{2} \times 3\sqrt{2} =$

9)   If $3x = 6$, what does $(3x + 2)^2 - 7 =$

10)	If $2x + 3y = 17$ and $x + 2y = 7$, then $(3x + 5y)/2 =$

11)	$7x - 4y = 24$ and $x + 12y = 40$, then $(x + y) =$

12)	If $x^2 - y^2 = 8$, then $2(x^2 - y^2) =$

13)	If $x = \frac{y}{5}$ and $10x = 14$, then $y =$

14)	If $(2 + 5) + (3 + x) = 7$, then $x =$

15) $\dfrac{7}{8} * \dfrac{8}{9} * \dfrac{9}{10} * \dfrac{10}{11} * \dfrac{11}{12} * \dfrac{12}{13} * \dfrac{13}{14} * \dfrac{14}{15} * \dfrac{15}{16} * \dfrac{16}{17} * \dfrac{17}{18}$

16) $5x - 2 = 13$
$x + y = 7$
$y = ?$

17) Eight (8) years ago my age was $\dfrac{1}{4}$ of what it will be in 16 years. How old am I?

18) If $x^2 = 25$ and $x > 0$, what is the sum of $x + 6 - (3x - 7)$?

19) If $\sqrt{81} + x = 324$, what is the value of x?

20) $c^{5/4} = 81$, what is $5c$?

21) Evaluate $(x^2 - 64) - (x^3 + 4x^2 - 14)$

22) A speedboat travels x miles in y minutes where $x = 16y\sqrt{y}$. What is the speed of the boat per hour?

23) Write the equation $(ax + 5)^2 = 49$ in factored form.

24) What is the quadratic formula?

25) What does the discriminant tell us about the number of solutions? What is the discriminant for:

- One solution?
- Two solutions?
- No solutions?

Unit 6: Absolute Value Equations

Notes:

1. Absolute value is indicated by straight brackets around a number $|x|$. It is defined as the distance a number is from 0 on a number line. The absolute value of $+7$ and -7 is the same (7).

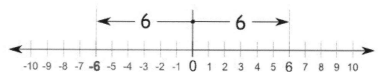

2. Absolute value may also be graphed on the coordinate plane.

   The parent graph is $|x| = 0$

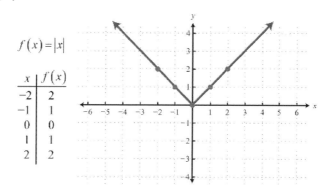

3. General Form of an Absolute Value Equation/Function

   $Y = a|x - h| + k$

   a = stretch or compression factor. Vertex is (h, k), the axis of symmetry is $x = h$

4. Absolute value graphs transform like other graphs do:
   1) $|x| - a$:   shifts a units down
   2) $|x| + a$:   shifts a units up
   3) $|x - a|$:   shifts a units right (opposite of its sign)
   4) $|x + a|$:   shifts a units left (opposite of its sign)
   5) $-|x|$:   flips over the x axis
   6) $y = a|x|$: $a > 1$, vertical stretch
   7) $y = a|x|$: $0 < a < 1$, compression
   8) $x \geq$ Shades above/inside the graphing lines, solid inequality line
   9) $x \leq$ Shades below the graphing lines, solid inequality line
   10) $x >$ or $x <$ Dotted line

Take the following steps in the absolute value equations below:

1) Solve algebraically.
2) Identify the stretch or compression factor, vertex and line of symmetry.
3) Identify the transformations from the absolute value parent graph.
4) Graph the equation on the coordinate plane provided.

1) $|x| - 4 = 0$

Algebraic work:

Stretch/Compression:

Transformation:

Line of Symmetry:

Vertex:

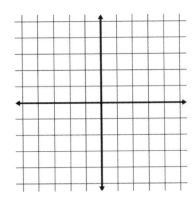

2) $|x + 3| - 1 = 0$

Algebraic work:

Stretch/Compression:

Transformation:

Line of Symmetry:

Vertex:

3) $-3|x + 1| + 5 = 0$

Algebraic work:

Stretch/Compression:

Transformation:

Line of Symmetry:

Vertex:

4) $\frac{1}{2}|x - 6| + 2 = 4$

Algebraic work:

Stretch/Compression:

Transformation:

Line of Symmetry:

Vertex:

5) $4 + |x + 2| = 7$

Algebraic work: Stretch/Compression:

Transformation: Line of Symmetry:

Vertex:

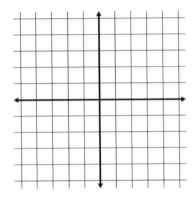

6) $6 - 5|x - 1| = 1$

Algebraic work: Stretch/Compression:

Transformation: Line of Symmetry:

Vertex:

Algebra Unit 7: Graphing: Lines, Quadratics, Cubes

Notes:

1. Linear Equations have the following forms and rules.

   $m = $ slope and $b = y$ intercept
   a. Standard: $ax + by = c$
   b. Slope Intercept: $y = mx + b$
   c. Point slope: $(y - y_1) = m(x - x_1)$
   d. Slope may be calculated using the following function: $(y_2 - y_1)/(x_2 - x_1)$
   e. Linear equations with identical slopes are parallel and never meet. Therefore, they have no solution.
   f. Linear equations with opposite (sign), reciprocal slopes are perpendicular and meet in exactly one point.

2. Quadratic Equations have the following forms
   a. Standard: $ax^2 + bx + c$
   b. Vertex: $a(x - h)^2 + k$, where (h, k) is the vertex
   c. Line of Symmetry: Based on standard form: $x = -b/(2a)$
   d. Vertex: L.O.S. x value, y value is evaluated by plugging x into the original standard form equation
   e. Minimum/Maximum: Vertex values
   f. $y = +x^2$ opens up. $y = -x^2$ opens down. $x = y^2$ opens right, $x = -y^2$ opens left

3. Equations with exponents of three or greater will generally be graphed on a calculator.

4. All graphs have parent functions.
   a. Linear: $y = x$
   b. Quadratic: $y = x^2$
   c. Cubic, etc.: $y = x^3$

5. Zeroes of functions are the x intercepts. To find the x intercepts, set $y = 0$, To find the y intercepts, set $x = 0$

6. Domain $=$ all x values. Range $=$ all y values

7. Cubic and equations of higher degrees will generally allow use of a calculator. If the questions refer to simple transformations, you will be expected to answer without a calculator.

8. Make yourself familiar with piecewise functions.

Linear Equation Practice Problems

Identify the slope, x intercept and y intercept AND graph the equation on the coordinate plane.

1)   (5, 2) and (6, -4)

Equation: X intercept: Y intercept:

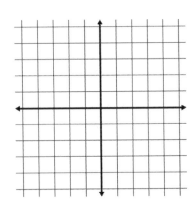

2)   (-5, 0) and (0, -5)

Equation: X intercept: Y intercept:

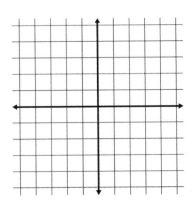

Quadratic Equation Practice Problems

Identify the vertex, the axis of symmetry, the maximum or minimum value, the range and domain of each quadratic equation below. Graph the equation on the coordinate plane.

3) $y = 6x^2 + 12x + 1$

Vertex: Axis of Symmetry: Minimum/Maximum:

Range: Domain:

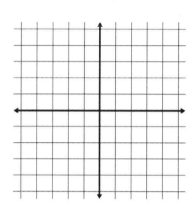

4) $y = 3(x - 3)^2 + 3$

Vertex: Axis of Symmetry: Minimum/Maximum:

Range: Domain:

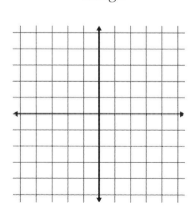

Linear and Quadratic Equation Word Problems

5) Suppose you are doing a 5000-piece puzzle. You have already placed 175 pieces. Every minute you place 10 more pieces.
   a. Write an equation in slope-intercept form to model the number of pieces placed. Graph the equation.
   b. After 50 more minutes, how many pieces will you have placed?

6) Suppose you have a $5-off coupon at a fabric store. You buy fabric that costs $7.50 per yard. Write an equation that models the total amount of money y you pay if you buy x yards of fabric. What is the graph of the equation?

7) The temperature at sunrise is 65°F. Each hour during the day, the temperature rises 5°F. Write an equation that models the temperature y, in degrees Fahrenheit, after x hours during the day. What is the graph of the equation?

8) A sailboat begins a voyage with **145**-lbs of food. The crew plans to eat a total of **15**-lbs of food per day.

    a. Write an equation in slope-intercept form relating the remaining food supply y to the number of days x.

    b. Graph your equation.

    c. The crew plans to have **25**-lbs of food remaining when they end their voyage. How many days does the crew expect their voyage to last?

9) A student government association wants to maximize profit selling mulch. The earnings can be modeled with the equation: $R = -2.5p^2 + 100p$. What price will earn the students the greatest gross profit?

10) A penny dropped from the Washington Monument (**555** feet tall) will fall in the model: $h = -16t^2 + 555$. How long will it take the penny to hit the ground?

11) On Mars, objects fall much more slowly than they do on earth. How long would a penny take to fall from the same height of 555 feet according to the model, $h = -6t^2 + 555$.

12) From 1990 through 2010, the number of iPhones sold can be approximated by the equation $.5c^2 - 5c + 7.8$ with the year $1990 = 0$. How many phones were sold in 2000 and in 2010?

Algebra Unit 8: Linear Systems

Notes:

There are four methods to solve linear systems:
1. Substitution
2. Linear Combination
3. Graphing
4. Matrices

With linear systems of one degree (exponent is **1**), there are **1, 0** or infinite solutions:
1. <u>One solution</u>: The lines cross at a single point on the graph.
2. <u>No solution</u>: The lines are parallel; they never cross. The slopes (m) are the same and the y-intercepts (b) are different.
3. <u>Infinite solutions</u>: The lines are the same. The slopes and the y-intercepts are the same.
   Note: These rules follow the discriminant rules (under notes in Chapter 5)

Determine if the ordered pair is a solution of the system.

1) $(4, -2)$
$$2x - 4y = 6$$
$$-x + 3y = 14$$

2) $(1, 0)$
$$6x - 2y = 6$$
$$-5x + 3y = -5$$

3) $(\frac{2}{3}, 0)$
$$-3x + 2y = 2$$
$$3x + 2y = -2$$

4) $(2, -1)$
$$-x + 2y = -4$$
$$-4x + 3y = -3$$

Solve all of the following problems twice (once with substitution and once with linear combination)

5) $x - 4y = 20$
       $2x + 5y = 1$

6) $9x - 5y = -30$
       $x + 5y = 18$

7) $x + 3y = -2$
       $-3x + y = 6$

8) $-x + y = -14$
       $2x - 3y = 33$

Graph the following equations and state the solution.

9) $2x + 3y = -7$
       $-4x - 5y = 13$

10) $2x - 2y = -8$
        $7x + 6y = 11$

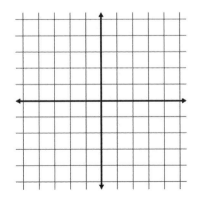

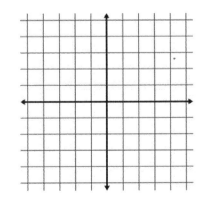

Use matrices to solve the following equations (calculator)

11) $x + y + 3z = 20$
$2x + 4y + 5z = 30$
$x + y + 4z = 26$

12) $3x - 6y + z = 0$
$3x - 4y - 4z = 15$
$-6x + 8y + 9z = -33$

13) $x + 2y - 6z = 23$
$x + 3y + z = 4$
$2x + 5y - 4z = 24$

14) $-x + 2y - 7z = -17$
$4x + 6y + 18z = 20$
$3x - y - 3z = -7$

Solve the following equations through substitution, combination or graphing

15) $x + \frac{3}{8}y = 1$
$8x + 3y = 4$

16) $.25x - 1.25y = 10.25$
$x - 5y = 20$

17) $\frac{1}{2}x + \frac{1}{3}y = 8$

$\frac{1}{4}x + \frac{1}{6}y = 12$

18) If: $3y - 4x = 5$

$2y - 3x = 10$

What is the value of $y - x$?

19) Find the value of $a - b$, if

$-2a - 5b = -15$ and

$3a + 4b = 19$

20) Find $3a - 2b$, if

$12 = 4a - 3b$ and

$7a = 5b - 2$

Graph the following equations and state the solution(s)

21) Tickets for a concert cost $10 each if you order them online, but you must pay a service charge of $8 per order. The tickets are $12 each if you buy them at the door on the night of the concert.

    a. Write a system of equations to model the situation. Let c be the total cost. Let t be the number of tickets.

    b. Graph the equation and find the intersection point. What does this point represent?

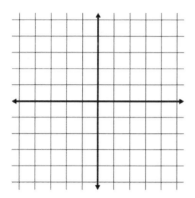

22) The number of right-handed students in a math class is nine times the number of left-handed students. The total number of students in the class is 30. How many right-handed students are in the class? How many left-handed students are in the class?

23) A rocket is launched from the Robinson launching field. It follows the path of $y = -x^2 + 5x$. At the same time, an arrow is shot in a linear path of $y = x + 6$. At what point do the rocket and arrow intersect? Solve algebraically and graph.

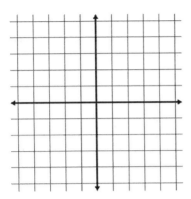

24) The price of AT&S stock can be modeled by the equation $y = .66x^2 - 10x + 25$. The price of Nerdizon stock has increased at a steady linear path of $y = 5x + 15$. When do the two stocks equal each other?

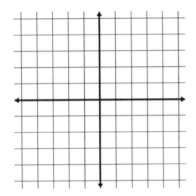

25) Alexander is bungee jumping. His jump can be modeled by the equation $h = -4.9t^2 + t + 360$. The bungee pulls back after several seconds which can be modeled at $h = -4t + 100$. After how many seconds did the bungee pull back?

Algebra Unit 9: Inequalities

Notes:

1. Inequalities are equations which represent greater than ($>$) or less than ($<$). A line underneath the $>$ or $<$ indicates greater than or equal to ($\geq$) or less than or equal to ($\leq$).

2. When you multiply or divide both sides of an inequality by a negative number, the greater than/less than sign flips directions.

Solve:

1) $3x + 5 \geq 4$

2) $5 \geq -\frac{1}{4}(x + 3)$

3) $-5x + 5 < 2(x - 4)$

4) $3 < 1 - 6x < 6$

5) $0 \leq \frac{1}{4}(x - 8) \leq 20$

6) $-8 < 1 - 3(x - 2) < 13$

7) If $a > b$, and $b > c$, define a in terms of c.

8) If $\frac{1}{x} > \frac{1}{5}$, solve for x

9) If $\frac{x}{3} + 2 > \frac{x}{2}$, solve for x

10) Ben's salary is greater than Jesse's, but less than Lynn's. If b, j, and l represent the salaries, write an inequality for the relationship.

Absolute Value Inequalities (Solve, graph and shade on a coordinate plane)

11) $|x - 10| \geq 17$

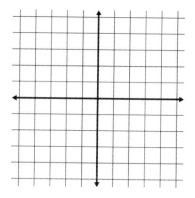

12) $|22x + 6| \leq 9$

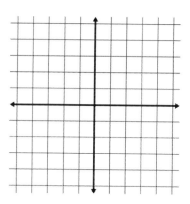

13) $|2x + 1| \leq 2$

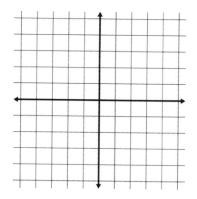

14) $|18 + \frac{1}{2}x| \geq 10$

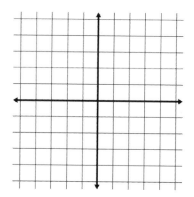

15) $\left|\dfrac{1}{4}p - \dfrac{1}{3}\right| \leq \dfrac{1}{3}$

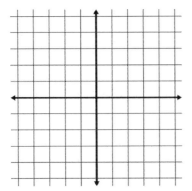

16) $\left|\dfrac{3}{5}x + 2\right| \geq 5$

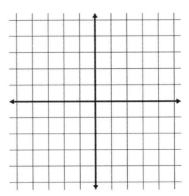

17) The ideal length of one type of model airplane is 90 cm. The actual length may vary from ideal by most 0.05 cm. What are the acceptable lengths for the model airplane?

18) The ideal circumference of a women's basketball is 28.75 in. The actual circumference may vary from the ideal by at most 0.25 in. What are the acceptable circumferences for a women's basketball?

19)   For safety, the recommended height of a horse fence is 5 ft. Because of uneven ground surfaces, the actual height of the fence can vary from this recommendation by up to 3 in. What are the maximum and minimum heights of the fence?

Algebra Unit 10: Fractions

Notes:

1. To add or subtract fractions, make sure to use a common denominator.

2. Fractions may be multiplied or divided without a common denominator.

3. Polynomials in fractions may only be cancelled AFTER factoring.

4. To prepare for this unit, STUDY long and synthetic division.

Solve:

1) $\frac{3}{8} + \frac{1}{8}$

2) $1\frac{8}{21} - \frac{15}{21}$

3) $9 - 3\frac{1}{2}$

4) $\frac{7}{6} - \frac{5}{18}$

5) $\frac{3}{5} * \frac{5}{8}$

6) $\frac{4}{9} * 2$

7) $\quad \frac{15}{16} * 3\frac{3}{5}$

8) $\quad -3\frac{1}{3} * (-1\frac{1}{5})$

9) $\quad (\frac{5}{8}) * (\frac{64}{9})/(\frac{3}{8})$

10) $\quad (\frac{2}{3})/(\frac{4}{9})/(\frac{1}{2})$

11) $\quad \frac{5x^2 + 10x - 15}{25x + 100}$

12) $\quad \frac{8x^2 - 4x}{16x^3}$

13) $\quad \frac{14x}{x^3} * \frac{2x^2}{7x^4}$

14) $\quad \frac{7x^4}{49x^2 + x^3}$

15) $\dfrac{2x}{x^2 + 2x + 1} \div \dfrac{x+1}{2x^2 + 2x}$

16) $\dfrac{x^2 - 6x - 7}{6x + 30} \div \dfrac{3x+15}{2x^2-50}$

17) $(2\frac{1}{3})/(3\frac{1}{4})$

18) $\dfrac{1}{4} + \dfrac{1}{2} / \dfrac{1}{3} + \dfrac{1}{4}$

19) $\dfrac{4\frac{1}{2} + 1\frac{2}{3}}{2\frac{1}{4} - 1\frac{3}{8}}$

20) $\dfrac{3\frac{1}{6} - 2\frac{1}{2}}{2\frac{5}{8}}$

Solve twice (once with long division and once with synthetic division):

21)　$(3x^3 - 5x^2 + 10x - 3) \div (3x + 1)$

22)　$(6x^5 + 4x^3 - x) \div (x - 1)$

23)　$(x^4 + 3x^3 + 7x^2 + 26x + 15) \div (x + 3)$

24)　$\dfrac{x^3 + 7x^2 + 15x + 9}{x + 1}$

Practice Problems:

25)　$x = \dfrac{2}{3}y$

　　　$y = \dfrac{3}{5}z$

　　Find x/z

26)　$\dfrac{3}{x} + \dfrac{2}{3} = \dfrac{5}{x}$

27) $\dfrac{x}{4} + \dfrac{7}{4} = \dfrac{-3}{x}$

28) $\dfrac{5}{x+6} = \dfrac{x-6}{5x}$

29) $x = \dfrac{7}{8}, y = \dfrac{9}{8}$ What is $\dfrac{x}{y}$?

30) If d and e are positive numbers and $\dfrac{de}{a-e} = 1$, what does $e = $?

31) Given $vz \neq k$, $z = \dfrac{1}{v}$, what does $(1-v)/(1-z) = $?

1) Simplify $\dfrac{2}{\frac{1}{d}-\frac{1}{e}}$

2) In a bowl of M & M candies, $\frac{1}{4}$ are green, $\frac{1}{3}$ are red, $\frac{1}{6}$ are yellow and $\frac{1}{12}$ are brown, what fractional part remains?

3) When a polynomial is divided by $(x-5)$, the quotient is $5x^2+3x+12$ with remainder 7. Find the polynomial.

4)   If the polynomial $x^3 + 6x^2 + 11x + 6$ expresses the volume, in cubic inches, of the box, and the width is $(x + 1)$ in., what are the dimensions of the box?

5)   Solve the linear system using substitution or linear combination.
$$3x - y = 7$$
$$2x + 3y = 1$$

6)   You buy a cd player for $150 and start to purchase cd's at $6.50 each. At what point will you have spent more on cd's than on the cd player?

7) Liam is considering two phone plans. Plan A offers a flat rate of $216 per month for unlimited calls, texting and data. Plan B offers a plan dependent on use. Calls and texting cost $50 per month. Phone rental is $37 per month. Data usage costs $17 per month per 2 GB of use. At what point are the two plans equal in cost.?

8) Find the solution of $y = x^2 - 6x + 8$ and $y = 3x + 2$. Graph the solution.

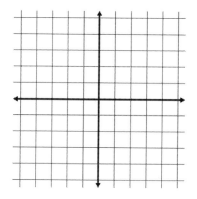

9) How many times do the following equations intersect?
$y = x^2 + 4$ and $y = 2$

10) Find the linear equality that has a slope of $\frac{1}{3}$ and a y-intercept of -2. The area above the line is shaded. What inequality should you write?

11) Meredith has $125,000 saved for medical school. If she will need to complete six years of medical school at a cost of $50,000 per year, how much will she have to borrow each year to have enough to finance her entire program?

12) Given the points (-7, 5) and (-5, -7), find the following:

Equation: X intercept: Y intercept:

13) Given the points (**1, 1**) and (**-1, -1**), find the following:

Equation: X intercept: Y intercept:

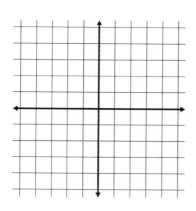

14) Solve: $7 - |2x + 6| - y = 4$

Algebraic work:

Transformation: Stretch/Compression:

Vertex: Line of Symmetry:

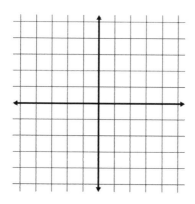

15) $|x + 8| - 6 \leq 2 + y$

Algebraic work:

Transformation: Stretch/Compression:

Vertex: Line of Symmetry:

Algebra Unit 11: Proportions, Ratios, Percentages, Growth & Decay

Notes:

1. Ratios and proportions may be written in three ways:

    $\frac{x}{y}$ $x : y$ x is to y

2. Percentages represent a proportion, a part to a whole, and based on 100.

3. <u>To change from a fraction to a percent:</u>
    a)   Divide to a decimal
    b)   Multiply by 100

    e.g.: $\frac{5}{8} = 0.625$

    $.625 * 100 = 62.5\%$

4. <u>To set up the percentage equation:</u>
    a) $\frac{is}{of} = \frac{\%}{100}$ or $\frac{part}{whole} = \frac{\%}{100}$
    b)   Cross-multiply and solve.

5. Simple Interest/Growth/Decay: $A = P(1 + rt)$
    A = future value, P = principal value, r = rate, t = time

6. Compound Interest: $A = P(1 + \frac{r}{n})^{nt}$ A = future value, P = principal value, r = rate, n = number of times the interest compounds per year, t = time in years.

7. Continuous Interest: $A = Pe^{rt}$ A = future value, P = Principal, e = integral that we use for continuous growth and decay; e is a function on your calculator. R = % rate, t = time.

8. Exponential growth has a base greater than 1.0 (ex. 2^x)

9. Exponential decay has a base less than 1.0 (ex. 0.85^x)

Set a ratio/fraction and simplify

1)   11 out of 121

2)   18 out of 27

3)   65 out of 200

4)   118 out of 354

Set as a unit rate

5)   364 miles on 9.2 gallons

6) $210 for 15 tickets

7)   18 inches of snow in 4 hours

8) $67,000 prize for 100 people

Solve for the variable

9) $\dfrac{3}{7} = \dfrac{m}{49}$

10) $\dfrac{6}{9.6} = \dfrac{x}{1.6}$

11) $\dfrac{r}{3} = \dfrac{8}{15}$

12) $\dfrac{7}{16} = \dfrac{x}{4.8}$

Express each fraction as a percent

13) $\dfrac{31}{100}$

14) $\dfrac{3}{8}$

15) $\dfrac{2}{3}$

16) $\dfrac{6}{5}$

Solve

17)　　40% of 60

18)　　60% of 40

19)　　7.5% of 80

20)　　110% of 20

21)　　16 is what percent of 40?

22)　　37 is what percent of 296?

23)　　$\frac{1}{2}$ is what percent of 8?

24)　　What percent of 400 is 2?

25)   28 is 20% of what number?

26)   19 is what percent of 76?

27)   16 is 40% of what number?

28)   21 is 35% of what number?

Word Problems

29)   How much interest is earned over 10 years on $2,000 with an 8% interest rate compounded:
    a)   Annually
    b)   Quarterly
    c)   Monthly
    d)   Daily
    e)   Continuously

30) How much interest is earned over 30 years on $242,000 with an 8% interest rate compounded:
   a) Annually
   b) Quarterly
   c) Monthly
   d) Daily
   e) Continuously

31) Dr. G. purchases a car for $32,000. If the car loses 15% of its value annually, how much is the car worth after 4 years?

32) If 10 fraternity members can mow the UVA lawn in twelve hours, how long would it take 6 sorority members?

33)   Julia put $122,000 into the stock market in 2005. The stocks lost money over a five-year period at the rate of **7.9%**. Find the values at:
        a) 1 year
        b) 3 years
        c) 5 years

34)   Jose is purchasing 4 dress shirts that cost $28 each and 2 pairs of pants that cost $38 each. The items are all on sale for **35%** off. How much money will Jose save by purchasing them on sale instead of at full price?

35)   A family sells a car to a dealership for **60%** less than they paid for it. They paid $9000 for the car. For what price did they sell the car?

Algebra Unit 12: Basic Statistics

Define:

1. Mean/Average: _____

2. Mode: _____

3. Median: _____

4. Scatter Plots: _____

Solve:

1)   Find the arithmetic mean, mode and median of the following data:
130, 155, 148, 184, and 172

2)   Find the arithmetic mean, mode and median of the following data:
25, 98, 30, 45, 36, 25, and 62

3)   What is the average of $\frac{3}{4}$, .64 and 1.87 in decimal/fraction form?

4)   The average of $2x - 1, 4, 6, 12$ and 13 is 9. What is the value of x?

5)   What is the average of: $x, x - 3, 2x - 5, 2x + 2$ and $1 - x$?

6)   The mean of x and y is 4. If $x = 5y$, what is y?

7)   What number must be added to $6, 16,$ and 8 to have an average of 13?

8)   After a fourth quiz, Kristin's English grade dropped from 98 to 95, what was her fourth quiz grade?

9)   Kelly earned a 92 on her first two tests and an 80 on her 3rd test. What will be her highest possible average after the 4th test?

10)   If $6x + 6y = 180$, what is the mean of x and y?

11)   The average of x, $2x - 8$, $2x + 2$, $3x - 1$, and $4x + 1$ is 6. What is the mode and median of these numbers?

12)   The average (arithmetic mean) of 1, 3, 6, 12, and x is 4. The average (arithmetic mean) of 2, 4 and y is 6. What is the value of $x + y$?

13)   The average (arithmetic mean) of a set of six numbers is 9. When a seventh number is added to the set, the average of the seven numbers is still 9. What number was added to the set?

Algebra Unit 13: Functions

Definitions

Relation: A set of ordered pairs (x, y).

Inputs: x values, also called domain.

Outputs: y values, also called range.

Function: A special type of relationship between two values in which each input value corresponds to exactly one output value. If two or more ordered pairs have the same x value, the relation is not a function. Functions must pass the vertical line test.

Notes:

Function Notation: A "normal" equation is written in standard from:
$$x + y = 5 \quad \text{or} \quad y = -x + 5$$
Written in function notation: $f(x) = -x + 5$

To Solve a Function: A function will be written in the following format: $f(x) = x - 9$
Find the indicated value of $f(3)$: $f(x) = x - 9$.
$$f(3) = 3 - 9$$
$$f(3) = -6$$

Function Operations: $f(x) = 3x$ and $g(x) = x - 5$

Addition: $f(x) + g(x) = 3x + (x - 5) = 4x - 5$

Subtraction: $f(x) - g(x) = 3x - (x - 5) = 3x - x + 5 = 2x + 5$

Multiplication: $f(x) * g(x) = 3x * (x - 5) = 3x^2 - 15x$

Division: $f(x) \div g(x) = (3x)/(x - 5)$

Composition of Two Functions:

$f(x) = 4x + 2$ and $g(x) = x - 3$ Find $f(g(x))$

Steps:
1) Substitute: $f(g(x)) = f(x - 3)$
2) Plug $g(x)$ into $f(x)$: $4(x - 3) + 2$
$$4x - 12 + 2$$
$$4x - 10 = f(g(x))$$

Inverse of Functions:

Written as $f(x)^{-1}$: the inverse of $f(x) = 4x + 2$

Steps:
1) Rewrite: $y = 4x + 2$

2) Change x and y: $x = 4y + 2$

3) Solve for y: $y = \frac{1}{4}x - \frac{1}{2}$

Solve:

1) Find the domain and range: $\{(1,5), (-2,8), (0,4), (-1,5), (2,8)\}$

2) Is the relation in #1 a function? Why or why not?

3) Find the domain and range: $\{(4,1), (7,2), (7,-2), (3,0), (4,-1)\}$

4)   Is the relation in #3 a function? Why or why not?

5)   Given $f(x) = 10x + 2$, find the value of $f(-1)$.

6)   Given $f(x) = -x^2 - 4x + 3$, find the value of $f(10)$.

Given $f(x) = 2x - 4$ and $g(x) = x - 1$, solve for $h(x)$

7) $h(x) = f(x) + g(x)$

8) $h(x) = f(x) - g(x)$

9) $h(x) = f(x) - 3g(x)$

10) $h(x) = \frac{1}{2}f(x) + 2g(x)$

11) $h(x) = f(x) * g(x)$

12) $h(x) = f(x) \div g(x)$

13) $h(x) = f(g(x))$

14) $h(x) = g(f(x))$

Find the inverses of the following functions

15) $f(x) = 11x + 22$

16) $f(x) = \frac{1}{2}(x - 10)$

17) $f(x) = x^2 - 1$

Algebra Unit 14: Imaginary Numbers

Notes:

For many students, who have always worked with real numbers, imaginary numbers are just incomprehensible! So what is an imaginary number? The square root of −1 is the basic unit of imaginary numbers, represented by i. $i = \sqrt{-1}$

The four basic math functions (addition, subtraction, multiplication and division) follow the basic rules of algebra that variables follow:

1. Different forms of i: Imaginary numbers may be represented in three ways:
   a) i
   b) $\sqrt{-1}$
   c) $i\sqrt{1}$ (the negative sign may be removed from the radical symbol and represented by an i in front of the radical sign). For example, $\sqrt{-6}$ may be represented by $i\sqrt{6}$.

2. Standard Form Equation: The standard form of an imaginary number equation is $a \pm bi$

3. Conjugate: The conjugate of the standard form of an imaginary number equation is also $a \pm bi$. The conjugate uses the opposite sign. For example, for the standard equation $a + bi$, the conjugate is $a - bi$.

4. Addition/Subtraction: Add or subtract coefficients. Examples:
   a) $i + 6i = 7i$
   b) $15i + 7i + 2 = 22i + 2$
   c) $46i - 52i + 9i = 3i$
   d) $-7 - 9 + 33i - 65i = -16 - 32i$

5. Multiplication/Division: Like all variables, imaginary numbers add or subtract exponents when like variables are multiplied or divided. As with variables, the coefficients multiply or divide separately from the variables' interactions. Examples:
   a) $6i * 7i = 42i^2$
   b) $5 * 8i * 2i^3 = 80i^4$
   c) $(32i^3)/(8i) = 4i$
   d) $(45i^6)/9i^9 = 5i^{-3}$ or $5/i^3$

6. Exponential Forms: The i, or basic unit of imaginary numbers, may grow exponentially into infinity. The ultimate value of the unit will also come down to four values:
   $i^1 = \sqrt{-1}$
   $i^2 = -1$
   $i^3 = -i$
   $i^4 = 1$

This pattern will repeat indefinitely. While *i* values may be computed on a calculator, students may also derive them through simple division. The steps include

a) Divide the imaginary number's exponent by 4. Ignore the coefficient.

b) The remainder will indicate what form of *i* will be left. Remainders may be decimals if using a calculator numbers 1-4 if using long division.

- A remainder of 1 or .25 will yield a value of *i* or $\sqrt{-1}$
- A remainder of 2 or .5 will yield a value of i^2 or -1
- A remainder of 3 or .75 will yield a value of i^3 or $-i$ or $-\sqrt{-1}$
- A remainder of 4 or 0.0 will yield a value of i^4 or 1

7. Negative Exponents: Imaginary numbers may be raised to negative exponents as well as to positive exponents as outlined above. When an imaginary number is raised to a negative exponent, the imaginary number will drop to the denominator of the fraction.

8. Rationalizing: Radicals, of any type, may NOT occur in the denominator of a fraction. Therefore, radicals which appear in the denominator of a fraction must be multiplied out to reach a single positive value or a polynomial with NO radicals. You will either multiply by *i* raised to an exponent (between 1 and 3) or by the conjugate of the binomial.

Solve (Rationalize denominators):

1) $\sqrt{-1} =$

2) $\sqrt{-36} =$

3) $\sqrt{-144x} =$

4) $\sqrt{-254} =$

5)   Find the conjugate of $a + bi$

6)   Find the conjugate of $a - bi$

7)   Find the conjugate of $5 - 6i$

8)   Find the conjugate of $6i + 5$

9) $(5 + 6i) + (6 - 3i) =$

10) $(18 + 2i) + (12 - 7i) =$

11) $(1 + 5i) - (3 - 2i) =$

12) $(11 + 25i) - (36 - 27i) =$

13) $\sqrt{-5} * \sqrt{7} =$

14) $\sqrt{9} * \sqrt{-9} =$

15) $i^6 * i^9 =$

16) $5i^6 * 7i^9 =$

17) $98i^6 * (1/14)i^2 =$

18) $75i^9/25i^8 =$

19) $144i^6/12i^4 =$

20) $(36 + 6i)/(6 + i) =$

21) $72/(6 * \sqrt{-7}) =$

22) $1/(4i^{-1}) =$

23) $(24i^{-5}) =$

24) $15i^{-2} =$

25) $5/(6 + i^3) =$

26) $(x^3 + 3x^2 + 4x + 12)/(x + 2i) =$

27) $(x^2 + 9)/(x + 3i) =$

28) $(x - 6i)^{-1} =$

29)   What is the quotient of $\frac{5-2i}{3+4i}$?

30)   Re rewrite the expression $(8-5i)^2$ in the form of $a+bi$.

31) $6x^2 - 5i^2 = 2x^2 - i^2$

32) $(5+5i) - 2i^2(1+3i) =$

33) $4i[3i(2 + i) - (3 - 9i)] =$

34) $7x^2 - 5 - 2x = 8x^2 + 5$

35) $-3x^2 - 5x - 3 =$

Algebra Unit 15: Basic Trigonometry

Notes:

Both the SAT and the ACT Exams will expect test-takers to have a basic understanding of trigonometry. This includes the two special trigonometric triangles (30-60-90) and (45-45-90) and the trigonometric unit circle. In this unit, we will introduce the two special triangles.

1.　　The foundation of trigonometry is triangles and the relationship of sides and angles.

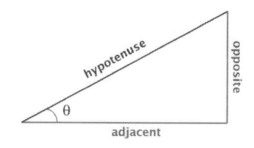

2.　　The two fundamental triangles ALWAYS follow specific ratios.

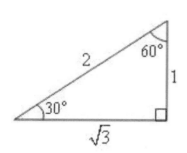　　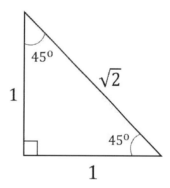

3.　　Sine, cosine and tangent are ratios of the triangles' legs divided by each other or by the hypotenuse. Students remember the ratios by the mnemonic: SOH–CAH–TOA. The mnemonic stands for:

Sine θ = opposite (leg) / hypoteneuse

Cosine θ = adjacent (leg) / hypotenuse

Tangent θ = opposite (leg) / adjacent (leg)

4. If you have not been exposed to trigonometry in school yet, try to memorize the chart below:

θ	0°	30°	45°	60°	90°
sin θ	0	$\dfrac{1}{2}$	$\dfrac{\sqrt{2}}{2}$	$\dfrac{\sqrt{3}}{2}$	1
cos θ	1	$\dfrac{\sqrt{3}}{2}$	$\dfrac{\sqrt{2}}{2}$	$\dfrac{1}{2}$	0
tan θ	0	$\dfrac{\sqrt{3}}{3}$	1	$\sqrt{3}$	undef.

Solve:

1) Evaluate the trigonometric functions for the triangle below.

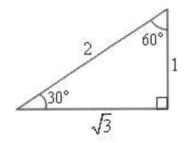

a) Sin 30° =

b) Cos 30° =

c) Tan 30° =

d) Sin 60° =

e) Cos 60° =

f) Tan 60° =

1) Evaluate the trigonometric functions for the triangle below.

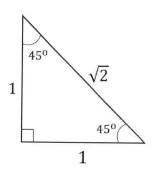

a)   Sin 45° =

b)   Cos 45° =

c)   Tan 45° =

2) Evaluate the trigonometric functions for the triangle below.

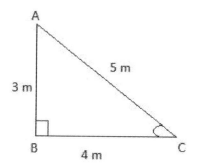

a)   Sin A =

b)   Cos A =

c)   Tan A =

d)   Sin C =

e)   Cos C =

f)   Tan C =

Draw a triangle for each of the following problems and find the sine, cosine and tangent for each question:

3)   Sin θ = 1/2   Cos: Tan:

4)   Sin θ = 1/3   Cos: Tan:

5)   Cosine θ = 15/17   Sin: Tan:

6)   Cosine θ = 5/13   Sin: Tan:

7)   Tan $\theta = 1/5$ Cos: Sin:

8)   Tan $\theta = 3/4$ Cos: Sin:

Mastery Unit C

1) The average of 6 and x is z. What is x in terms of 6 and z?

2) If 12 students earned an average grade of **88** on a test and **8** other students earned an average of **91**, what would the average of the whole group be?

3) After purchasing a gross (**144**) of candy kisses, a woman eats **12**, what percent is left?

4) An 80-gallon baby pool is **60%** full. If the water is then poured into a 60-gallon baby pool, what percent of the smaller pool is filled?

5) If a co-ed dorm houses 40% men and there are 120 women, how many men are in the dorm?

6) A fast food egg machine can make 60 eggs in nine seconds, how many eggs can it make in six minutes?

7) In cleaning out her closet, Joanne notices that the ratio of jeans to dress pants to skirts is 2 : 5 : 7. If she has a total of 140 dress pants, skirts and jeans, how many pairs of jeans does she have?

8) Find the inverse of the function $f(x) = -\frac{2}{3}x + 1$

9)   Simplify i^7.

10)   If David's goal is to retire with **$1,450,000** at the age of **62** and he is earning interest at the rate of **11%**, how much money must he invest at the age of:
       a)   32
       b)   42
       c)   52

11)   If **9** students can clean a school in **12** hours, how long would it take **3** students?

12)   If $\sin\theta = \frac{3}{5}$, what is the value of $\cos\theta$ and $\tan\theta$?

13) If the scale on a topographical map indicates that two inches equals 86 miles, how many miles would be represented by 4.3 inches?

14) If $f(x) = 2x + 1$ and $g(x) = x^2 - 3x + 4$, find:
a) $(f * g)(x)$
b) $(f + g)(x)$
c) $(f - g)(x)$

15) In a triangle ABC, the measure of $\angle B$ is $90°$, $BC = 12$, and $AC = 13$. Triangle DEF is similar to triangle ABC, where vertices D, E, and F correspond to vertices A, B, and C, respectively, and each side of triangle DEF is $\frac{1}{4}$ the length of the corresponding side of triangle ABC. What is the value of $\sin F$?

16) If snow is falling at the rate of 4.3 flakes per second, how many flakes will have fallen after 2.5 days?

17)   What is the quotient of $\frac{3+2i}{4+6i}$?

18)   In right triangle JKL, the measure of $\angle L$ is $90°$, hypotenuse $JK = 5$ units, and side $KL = 2$ units. What is $\tan K$?

19)   If a fast food fryer cooks 9,600 French fries per hour:
       a)   How many fries are cooked in a minute?
       b)   How long will it take to cook 800 fries?

20)   If $f(x) = 2x + 4$ and $g(x) = -x^2 + 5$, find $f(g(x))$ and $g(f(x))$.

21) Simplify $\left(\frac{1}{1-i}\right)^2$.

22) If the $\tan \theta = 1$, what is the value of $\sin \theta$?

23) If $f(x) = 4x^2 + 2x + 2$, find $f(2)$ and $f(-5)$.

24) A sports utility vehicle holds 35 gallons of gas and is $\frac{5}{7}$ full. How much will it cost to fill the tank at \$2.85 per gallon?

25) In a right triangle, one angle measures $x°$, where $\cos x° = \frac{3}{5}$. What is $\sin(90° - x°)$?

26) Simplify $(5i)^2$.

27) The ratio of x to 7 is 49 to 343. What is x?

28) The area of a right triangle is 50. One of its angles is 45°. Find the lengths of the sides and hypotenuse of the triangle.

29) If $f(x) = 3x + 1$, find $f^{-1}(7)$.

30) Julia props up a ladder against a wall. The ladder makes an angle of $25°$ from the ground. If the ladder is 12 feet long, which of the following is the expression for finding the distance the foot of the ladder is from the wall?

   a) $12 \cos 25°$
   b) $\sin \frac{10}{25}$
   c) $\cos \frac{10}{25}$
   d) $12 \sin 25°$
   e) $12 \tan 25°$

31) Find the future value of $10,000$ compounded at a rate of 5%
   a) Over 5 years, annual compounding
   b) Over 5 years, quarterly compounding
   c) Over 5 years, continuous compounding

32) In right triangle ABC, if $\sin A = 0.5$ and side $BC = 10$, find the length of the hypotenuse, AB, and side AC.

33) Multiply and simplify $3i(1 + 5i)(-3 - i)$, write in the form of $a + bi$.

34) The population of the United States in the year 1980 was 227,224,681. If the population grows at a continuous rate of 0.9%, what will the population be in 1990?

35) Let the function f be defined by $f(x) = 6x - 3a$, where a is a constant. If $f(10) + f(5) = 60$, what is the value of a?

36)   Emma and Meredith's dinner bill came to $76.32, not including a 20% tip. If they split the total bill with tax in half, how much did each owe?

Geometry

The following geometry review is divided into 4 units of study. Each unit begins with a review of definitions and properties. Practice problems are also included in each unit.

Since the problems can be used for further review, write neatly and SHOW your work. Answers for each problem are provided in Chapter 6.

Geometry Unit 1: Angles

Definitions & Properties:

<u>Angle:</u> An angle is made up of two rays that have the same initial point. The initial (meeting) point of the rays is the vertex of the angle. An angle may be named by is vertex (single point) or by its three points, e.g.:

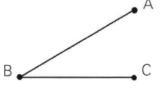

Angle B

Angle CBA

Angle ABC

<u>Classifying Angles</u>: Angles are classified by their degree measure:

Acute Angle:	Angle of $< 90°$
Right Angle:	Angle of $90°$
Obtuse Angle:	Angle of $> 90°$ but $< 180°$
Straight Angle:	Angle of exactly $180°$
Complementary Angles:	Two angles that add to $90°$
Supplementary Angles:	Two angles that add to $180°$
Linear Pair:	Two angles that form a straight angle, adding to $180°$
Congruent Angles:	Angles with equal degree measure

Special Formations of Angles:

<u>Angle Bisector:</u> A line or line segment that divides an angle exactly in half at the angle's vertex, creating two equal angles.

<u>Perpendicular Lines:</u> Perpendicular lines and line segments from right angles ($90°$), denoted by:

<u>Parallel Lines:</u> Two or more lines in the same plane that never meet, have equal slopes, and remain equidistant from each other for infinity. When parallel lines are cut by a transversal, they form a series of specially defined angles.

<u>Transversal:</u> A line that cuts 2 or more parallel lines.

Congruent Angles Formed by Parallel Lines Cut by a Transversal:

If two or more parallel lines are intersected by a transversal, special angle relationships are formed.

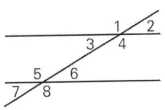

Corresponding Angles:

Angles that are in similar positions are equal:

Angles 1 & 5   Angles 2 & 6

Angles 3 & 7   Angles 4 & 8

Alternate Interior Angles:

Angles that are in similar positions inside the parallel lines, are opposite of each other and have equal degree measure:

Angles 3 & 6   Angles 4 & 5

Same Side Interior Angles:

Same side interior angles are supplementary (= 180°):

Angles 4 & 6   Angles 3 & 5

Alternate Exterior Angles:

Angles that are in similar positions outside the parallel lines, are opposite of each other and have equal degree measure:

Angles 1 & 8   Angles 2 & 7

Same Side Exterior Angles:

Same side exterior angles are supplementary (= 180°):

Angles 1 & 7   Angles 2 & 8

Vertical Angles:

Angles that form an "X" and are opposite each other:

Angles 1 & 4   Angles 2 & 3

Angles 5 & 8   Angles 6 & 7

***NOTE:** The angles delineated above are only equal if the two (or more lines) cut by the transversal are parallel. The SAT problem must specify that the lines are parallel!!!

Practice Problems

1)   Given: Line A is parallel to line B

Lines A and B are cut by the transversal, line C

$\angle 2 = 42°$

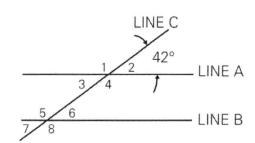

What are the measures of these angles?

$\angle 1 =$ $\angle 5 =$

$\angle 2 = 42°$ $\angle 6 =$

$\angle 3 =$ $\angle 7 =$

$\angle 4 =$ $\angle 8 =$

2)   If $\angle 1 = Y°$, in terms of Y, what is the measure of each angle?

$\angle 1 = Y°$ $\angle 3 =$

$\angle 2 =$ $\angle 4 =$

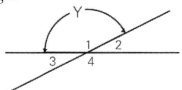

Figure not drawn to scale

3)   Given: Line P is parallel to Line N

Lines P and N are cut by the transversal, Line M

$\angle 6 = 2X + 10°$

$\angle 8 = 5X - 40°$

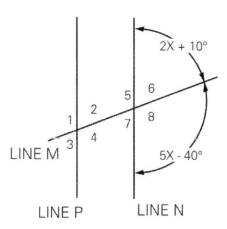

What are the measures of the following angles?

$\angle 1 =$ $\angle 5 =$

$\angle 2 =$ $\angle 6 =$

$\angle 3 =$ $\angle 7 =$

$\angle 4 =$ $\angle 8 =$

4)   Given: $\angle A = 140°$

$\angle E = 155°$

What are the measures of the following angles?

$\angle A = 140°$ $\angle E = 155°$

$\angle B =$ $\angle F =$

$\angle C =$ $\angle G =$

$\angle D =$ $\angle H =$

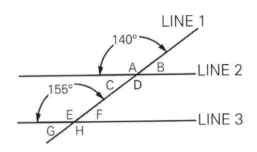

5)   Given: $\angle GOF = 36°$

$\angle BOD = 90°$

Line EA bisects $\angle BOH$

What are the measures of angles:

$\angle FOE =$ $\angle AOH =$

$\angle EOD =$ $\angle HOG =$

$\angle DOC =$ $\angle GOE =$

$\angle COB =$ $\angle BOH =$

$\angle BOA =$

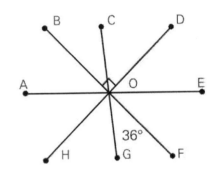

6)   What is the measure of angle AOB?

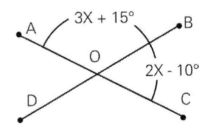

7) Given: Line M is parallel to Line N

What is the measure of the larger of the two angles?

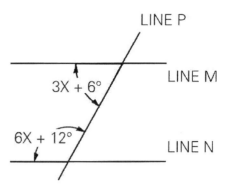

LINE P

LINE M

$3X + 6°$

$6X + 12°$

LINE N

Figure not drawn to scale

8) Given: Line N is parallel to Line P

What is the measure of ∠ABC?

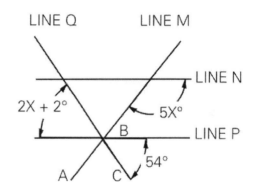

LINE Q   LINE M

LINE N

$2X + 2°$ $5X°$

B   LINE P

$54°$

A   C

9) Two angles are complementary. If one angle equals 31°, what is measure of the sum of the angles?

10) Given: $\angle BOC = 58°$

$\angle COD$ is bisected by a line N

What is measure of ∠BOA? _____

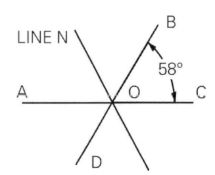

LINE N   B

$58°$

A   O   C

D

Figure not drawn to scale

Geometry Unit 2: Triangles

Definitions:

Triangle: A 3-sided closed figure, named by its vertices (points where two sides meet). e.g.:

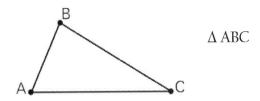

Δ ABC

Vertex: The common endpoint of two of sides of a triangle.

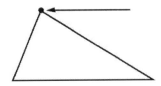

Leg: A side of a triangle (non-hypotenuse and non-base).

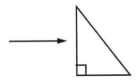

Base: In an isosceles triangle, the third non-congruent side of a triangle.

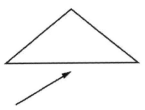

Hypotenuse: In a right triangle, the side opposite the right angle.

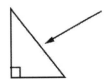

Altitude: A perpendicular segment connecting the vertex and its non-included side.

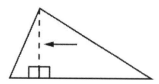

Median: A segment with endpoints are the vertex of a triangle and the midpoint of the opposite side.

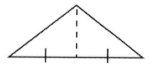

Perimeter: The sum of the lengths of the three sides of a triangle.

Area: The number of square units needed to cover a surface.

Area of a $\Delta = \frac{1}{2}$ base * height

Note: Some triangles need an altitude to compute area.

Properties:

1.   The sum of the angles in a triangle is always 180°.

2.   There can be at most one right or one obtuse angle in a triangle.

3.   Size of the angle controls the length of the sides. Longer sides are across from larger angles and smaller sides are across from smaller angles.

4.   The sum of the measures of two sides of a triangle may not equal more than the measure of the third side.

5.   Exterior angles are formed by extending one of the sides.

6.   The exterior angle is equal to the sum of the two remote angles in the triangle.

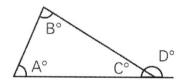

The exterior angle (D) is equal to the sum of the two remote interior angles (A + B).

Pythagorean Theorem: In a right triangle, the sum of the squares of the measures of the legs equals the square of the measure of the hypotenuse: $a^2 + b^2 = c^2$

<u>Pythagorean Triplets:</u>

3 – 4 – 5
5 – 12 – 13
8 – 15 – 17
7 – 24 – 25

** These triplets may be multiplied by any common factor and remain Pythagorean triplets.

Classifying Triangles: Triangles may be classified by their sides and/or their angles.

<u>By Sides:</u>   <u>Scalene Δ</u>: Has no congruent sides

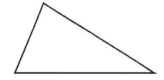

<u>Isosceles Δ</u>: Has two congruent sides, called legs

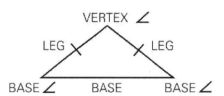

<u>Equilateral Δ</u>: Has three congruent sides and three congruent angles

<u>By Angles:</u>   <u>Acute Δ</u>: Has three angles with measures of $< 90°$

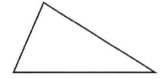

<u>Right Δ</u>: Has one angle of **90°**, formed by two perpendicular sides.

<u>Obtuse Δ</u>: Has one angle with measure of **>90°**

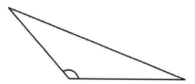

<u>Equiangular Δ</u>: Has three equal angles and three equal sides.

<u>Similar Triangles</u>:   All six parts of one triangle will be in the same ratio to all six parts of another triangle.

<u>Congruent Triangles</u>:   All six parts (three angles and three sides) of one triangle must be congruent to all six parts of another triangle.

Methods of Proving Congruency:

<u>Side-Side-Side (SSS)</u>:   The three sides of one triangle must be congruent to the three sides of another triangle.

<u>Side-Angle-Side (SAS)</u>:   Two sides and the angle between the two sides must be congruent to the two sides and their included angle of another triangle.

Angle-Side-Angle (ASA):	Two angles and the included side of one triangle must be congruent to two angles and the included side of the other triangle.

Angle-Angle-Side (AAS):	Two angles and a non-included side of one triangle must be congruent to the corresponding two angles and side of the other triangle.

Angle-Side-Side (ASS):	This proof never works – ever!!!! Do not be fooled!!!

2 Angles:	If two angles of a triangle are congruent then the third angle of the triangles is congruent. Thus, the two triangles are similar, but not necessarily congruent.

Special Ratios of Congruency:

Perimeter:	The perimeter of two congruent triangles will have the same ratio as the two perimeters.

Area:	The ratio of the areas of two congruent triangles is the square of the ratio of the sides.

Special Right Triangles:

Special right triangles form the basis of trigonometry. The two special right triangles used in the SAT will be the 30° – 60° – 90° triangle and the 45° – 45° – 90° triangle. These two right triangles will always preserve the same angle/side ratios.

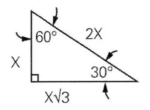 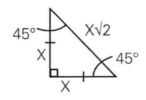

Practice Problems

Find the missing variable(s). Classify the triangles by their angles and their sides. Note: The figures are not drawn to scale.

1)

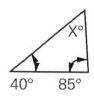

6)

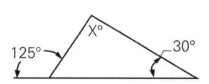

2)

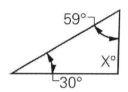

7)

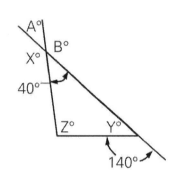

3)

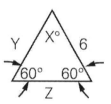

8)

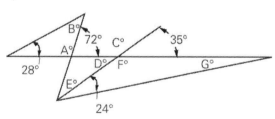

A =
B =
C =
D =
E =
F =
G =

4)

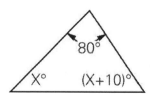

5)

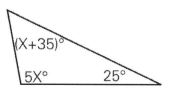

9)   Given $\angle J = \angle K$

Angles:

A =
B =
C =
D =
E =
F =
G =
H =
I =
J =
K =

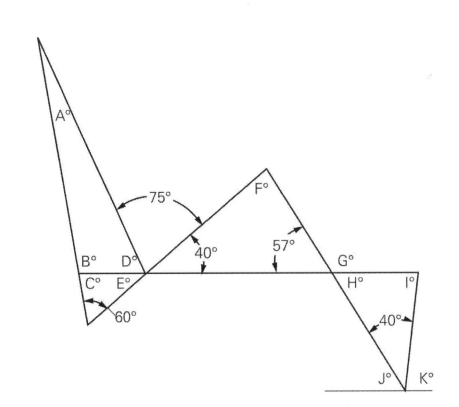

10)

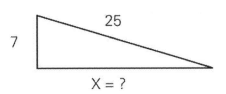

X = ?

11)

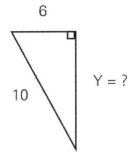

Y = ?

Classify the following triangles by their sides and angles and determine congruency

12)

13)

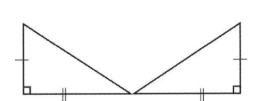

14) *Given* $\triangle XYZ \approx \triangle ABC$

$\angle Y = 57°$

$\angle A = 64°$

$\angle Z = (5t + 4)°$

Solve for t.

15) What is value of ∠ ABC?

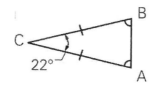

16) Given equilateral $\triangle FGH$ with side FG = 8, what is the area of the triangle?

17) Find the area of $\triangle BCD$.

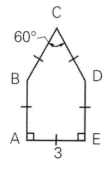

18) Area of $\triangle$ FGH = 12 inches²

Solve for x

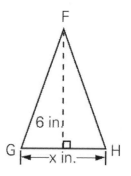

19) Find the area of an equiangular triangle whose perimeter is 48 inches.

20)   Solve for Y/2 if the area of the following triangle is 48 square inches.

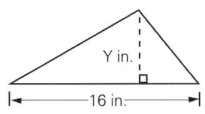

21)

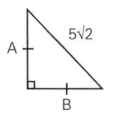

22)   Solve for A, X, and Y

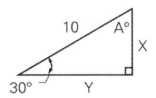

23)

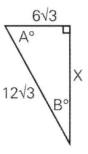

24)   Find the value of all 3 angles and the remaining two sides.

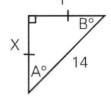

25)   If the perimeter of the triangle at the left is $6 + 3\sqrt{2}$, what is the value of:

X =
Y =
A =
B =
Area of the triangle =

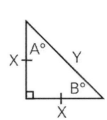

26) Given EBCD is a square, what is the area of the entire polygon?

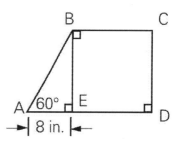

27) What is the value of $(X + Y)°$

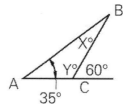

28) Given two equilateral triangles, A and B, what is the ratio of the sides of ΔA to ΔB?

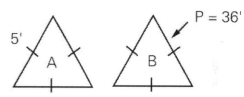

Figures not drawn to scale

29) What is the value of $X^2 + Y^2$?

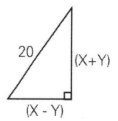

30) The perimeter of Δ B is 30 units. The perimeter of Δ A is 6 units, what is the ratio of their areas?

31) Given the perimeter of the Δs is equal, what is the length of side RS?

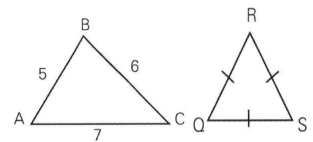

32) Find the measures of angles:

A =
B =
C =
D =
E =
F =
G =

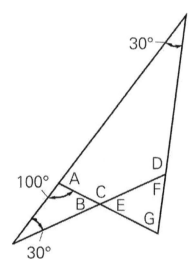

Geometry Unit 3: Polygons with 360° or more

Definitions & Properties:

Polygon: A closed (concave, non-convex) figure with three or more sides, formed with a finite number of coplanar segments. Polygons are classified by the relationship of their sides and angles.

Regular Polygon: Also called a convex polygon, all sides and angles are congruent.

Quadrilateral: A polygon which has four sides and four angles.

Parallelogram: A quadrilateral with the following characteristics:
1) Two pairs of parallel sides
2) Opposite sides are congruent
3) Diagonals bisect each other
4) Same side angles are supplementary

Rectangle: A parallelogram with the following characteristics:
- Four right (90°) angles
- Congruent diagonals

Rhombus: A parallelogram with the following characteristics:
- All sides congruent
- Diagonals are perpendicular
- Diagonals bisect each other
- Diagonals bisect opposite angles

Trapezoid: A quadrilateral with exactly one pair of parallel sides called bases. If the legs are congruent, the trapezoid is called isosceles.

Square: A parallelogram with all sides congruent and all angles congruent (right and 90°).

Pentagon: A polygon with five sides

Hexagon: A polygon with six sides

Heptagon: A polygon with seven sides

Octagon: A polygon with eight sides

Nonagon: A polygon with nine sides

Decagon: A polygon with ten sides

Sides/Angles: Any regular polygon has the same number of sides and angles, e.g., a square has 4 sides and 4 angles

| No. of Triangles: | To compute the number of triangles in any polygon: |
| | Number of sides $- 2$ |

| Total Degrees: | To compute the total degrees in any polygon: |
| | (Number of sides $- 2) * 180$ or $(n - 2) * 180$ |

| Angle Measure: | To compute the measure of each individual angle in a polygon, begin with the equation above and secondly divide the result by the number of sides/angles in the polygon. |

$$\frac{(n-2)*180}{n}$$

Formulas

Area of most quadrilaterals: base $*$ height $=$ units^2

Area of trapezoids: $\frac{1}{2}$ height (base$_1$ + base$_2$) $=$ units^2

Volume of most polygons: area of base $*$ height $=$ units^3

Practice Problems

1)   Find the total angle measure of each figure:

      a.   Triangle

      b.   Quadrilateral

      c.   Rhombus

      d.   Pentagon

      e.   Hexagon

      f.   Heptagon

      g.   Octagon

      h.   Nonagon

      i.   Decagon

2)   What is the measure of the fourth angle in a quadrilateral if the others are $40°$, $100°$, and $70°$?

3)   Find the measure of the smallest angle of a quadrilateral if the total interior angle measure equals $x + 5, x + 8, \ x + 20,$ and $x + 35$.

4)   One angle of a parallelogram $= 38°$, find the other three angles.

5)   Find the diagonals, perimeter and area of square with sides of 24 feet.

6)   Find the measure of A and B in the parallelogram below.

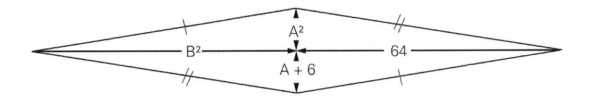

7)   How many triangles are in an octagon?

8)   Find the area of figure DEFG.

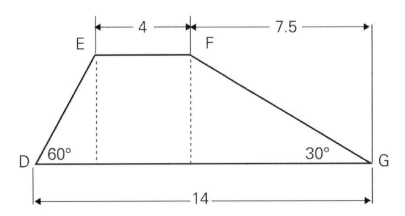

9)   If ABCDEF is a regular hexagon, what is the value of ∠FAB?

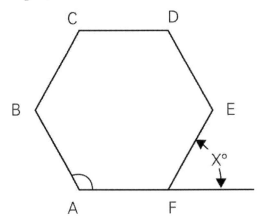

10)   What is the value of ∠X in the hexagon in problem number 9?

11)   Find the area and perimeter of the figure below.

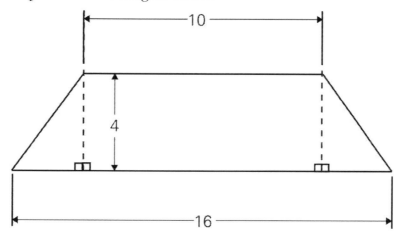

12)   The area of an isosceles trapezoid is 36 cm². Its perimeter is 28 cm and one leg is 5 cm, what is its height?

13)   ABCD is a square with diagonals intersecting at E. AB = 3. What is:
        a)   AC
        b)   DE

14) MNOP is a rectangle, QMRN is a rhombus. Find:

    a)   ∠ NQM

    b)   ∠ MRO

    c)   ∠ ORP

    d)   ∠ NPO

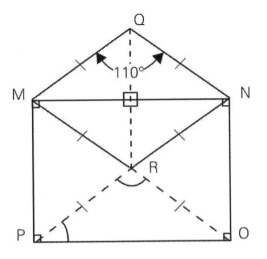

15) Given ABCD is a square, find the length of BC given that:

    a) $AB = 1 + 10x$
    b) $CD = 13 + 3x$

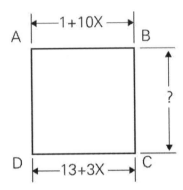

Geometry Unit 4: Circles

Definitions & Properties:

Circle: A set of points that consists of all points in a plane that are equidistant from the center of a circle.

Naming: A circle is named by its center.

Circle A:

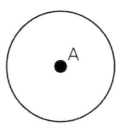

Radius: Line segment with one endpoint at the center of a circle and one endpoint on the circle itself.

Radius AB:

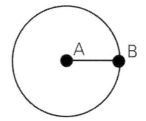

Chord: A line segment whose endpoints are on the circle, but not necessarily through the center.

Chord CD:

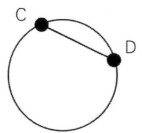

Diameter: A chord that goes through the center of the circle, the longest possible chord in a circle.

Diameter EF:

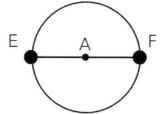

Degree Measure:	360°

Central Angle:	An angle whose vertex is at the center of the circle. May measure between 0° and 360°.

Central Angle GAH:

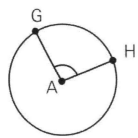

Arcs:	An unbroken part of a circle, created by a central angle. Arc GH is created by central angle GAH.

Arc GH:

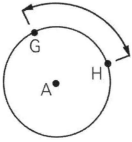

Minor Arc:	An arc with measure of less than 180°.

Minor Arc IK:

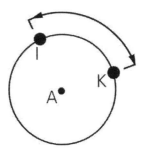

Major Arc:	An arc with measure of more than 180°.

Major Arc LMN:

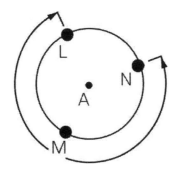

| Semicircle: | The arc (½ circle) created by a **180°** central angle. |

Semicircle OAP:

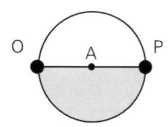

| Sector: | A pie-shaped piece of a circle formed by a central angle and an arc. |

Sector RAS:

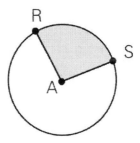

| Circumference: | Linear distance around a circle. The units are always linear (not squared or cubed). |

$C = 2 * \pi * \text{radius}$ or $\pi * \text{diameter}$
$2\pi r$ or πD

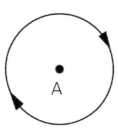

| Area of a Circle: | The number of square units within a circle. |

$A = \pi * \text{radius}^2$ or $A = \pi \left(\frac{1}{2}D\right)^2$

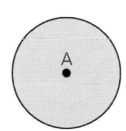

Arc Length: Linear distance of the arc. The length of the arc is the part of the circumference
                           proportional to the measure of the central angle to 360°.

$$\frac{\text{Arc length}}{\text{Circumference}} = \frac{\text{Central angle}}{360°}$$

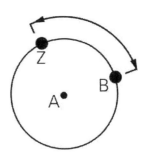

Area of a sector: Number of square units within a sector of a circle. The area of the sector is
                           proportional to the area of the circle.

$$\frac{\text{Sector area}}{\text{Area of circle}} = \frac{\text{Central angle}}{360°}$$

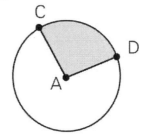

Concentric Circle: Two or more circles, one within the other(s), sharing the same center.

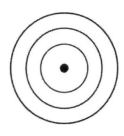

Pi: Represented by the symbol π. Its value is approximately 22/7 or 3.14159...

Volume of a cylinder: $\pi *$ radius$^2 *$ height

$$\pi r^2 h$$

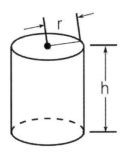

Practice Problems

1)   Given Circle A:

    a.   Name all chords.

    b.   Name two diameters.

    c.   Name four radii.

    d.   Name a chord that is not a diameter.

    e.   If DA = 5, what is EB?

    f.   Find the circumference of Circle A if EB = 8.

    g.   Find the area of Circle A if DF = 12.

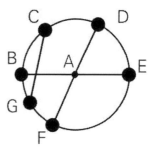

2)   Given Circle B, find:

    a)   Circumference of the circle.

    b)   Area of the circle.

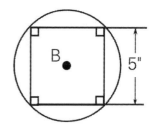

3)   Given Circle C, find:

    a)   Area of the circle.

    b)   Area of the shaded region.

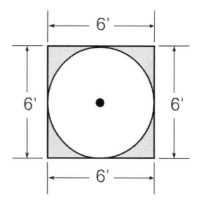

4)   Given Circle D, find:

    a)   Area of the circle.

    b)   Circumference of the circle.

    c)   Find the area of the circle, not included in the rectangle.

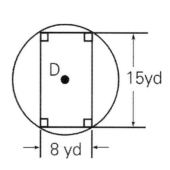

5)   Given Circle E, find:

    a)   Area of the circle

    b)   Area of the triangle.

    c)   Perimeter of the triangle

    d)   Area of the circle, not included in the triangle.

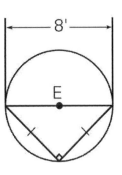

6)   Given Circle A, find the measures of the following angles:

    a)   ∠ CAD

    b)   ∠ DAE

    c)   ∠ FAE

    d)   ∠ FAB

    e)   ∠ BAC

    f)   ∠ CAF

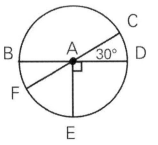

7)   If $AC = 6$ cm in Circle A (above), find the measures of the following arcs:

    a)   CD

    b)   DE

    c)   FB

    d)   BE

    e)   FC

8) If AC = 7 cm in Circle A (above), find the area of the following sectors:

   a) CAD

   b) DAF

   c) FAB

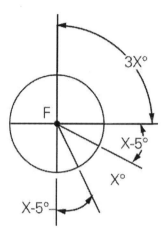

9) Given Circle F, find the measures of the smallest and largest angles.

10) If the radius of a circle is tripled, what happens to the circumference and the area?

11) If the area of a circle is 36π inches2, what is the area of a sector created by a central angle of 60°?

12) Find the thickness of a tire whose outer radius is 8 inches and whose inner radius is $5\frac{3}{8}$ inches.

13)   If a horse is tethered to a fence post at an angle of 90°, and his lead line is 15 feet long, over how many square feet can he graze?

14)   If a soda can has a radius of 1.5 inches and a height of 6 inches, what is its volume?

15)   If a circular baby pool is 4 feet across and 12 inches high, what is its volume?

16)   If a tire of diameter of 30 inches travels two miles (mile = 5280 feet),

    a)   How many linear feet does it cover?

    b)   How many revolutions does the tire make in its travel?

17)   Find the smallest and largest angles of Circle G.

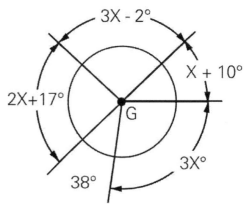

18) If the circumference of Circle H is three times the circumference of Circle I and the length of HI is 18 inches, what is the diameter of Circle I?

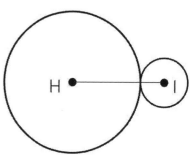

19) If the measure of JK equals 8 feet, what is the area of the shaded region?

Given ∠A = 90°

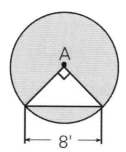

20) What is the ratio of the area of Circle M to the area of Circle N?

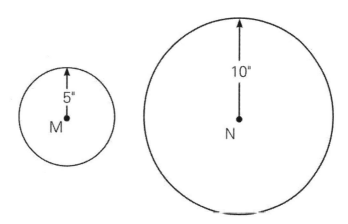

y other D

m v. The strong

om v and put them onto

$$\left[\cdots D^T\left(\frac{\partial F}{\partial Du}\right)\right]v\,dx\,dy.$$

EXAMPLE 2

the derivatives

denominator. The

$$-\frac{d}{dx}(1 +$$

every term in these equat

the book *the framework* be

$$u \longrightarrow e =$$

of odd order (with an odd number of

derivatives it is $D^T = \cdots + D_r$

of variations, is the real source of $A^T C A$. The

Du is between, C can be nonlinear. Normally it is

$\frac{1}{2}(Du)^2$, then $D^T \partial F/\partial Du$ becomes $D^T(cDu)$—

before testing it on examples.

of variations can be stated in three equivalent

Minimize $E[u] = \iint_S F(u)\,dx\,dy$

$$\iint_S \left(\sum \frac{\partial F}{\partial Du}\right)(D_Pu)\,dx\,dy = 0 \quad \text{for all } v$$

$$\left(\frac{\partial F}{\partial Du}\right) = 0.$$

and its derivatives.

Chapter 6

Math Answers

In this chapter:

- Algebra Answers

- Geometry Answers

Algebra Answers

Unit 1 – Arithmetic

Define:

Sum:	Addition, +
Difference:	Subtraction, −
Product:	Multiplication, × or ∗
Quotient:	Division, ÷
Factors:	Two or more numbers multiplied together to form a product
Digit:	Any of the Arabic numbers: 0, 1, 2, 3, 4, 5, 6, 7, 8, 9
Integers:	Any of the natural numbers, the negatives of these numbers, or 0. Example: ... -5, -4, -3, -2, -1, 0, 1, 2, 3, 4, 5 ...
Whole Numbers:	Positive integers, not including 0

1) 2,367

2) 3,207

3) 25,427

4) 22,134

5) 18,988

6) 28,079

7) 920

8) 285

9) 414

10) 538,200

11) 5,672,249

12) 1,850,618

13) 221,125

14) 507,936

15) 2532.4

16) 126

17) 64

18) 0

19) undefined

PEMDAS: Parentheses, Exponents, Multiplication or Division (whichever comes first in the equation), Addition or Subtraction (whichever comes first in the equation)

20) 50

21) 15

22) 35

23) 243

24) 0

25) 20

26) $14 - 5 \times 3 + 3^2$

Unit 2 – Polynomials

Define:

Variable: A letter that is used to represent 1 or more numbers

Monomial: Polynomial expression with only 1 term

Binomial: Polynomial with 2 terms that may be added or subtracted

Trinomial: Polynomial with 3 terms that may be added or subtracted

Numerical Coefficient: Numerical part of a term that contains a variable

Base: Number or variable used as factor multiplied using exponent

Exponent: Superscript that indicates how many times a base is multiplied

Addition and Subtraction of Polynomials

1) $y^2 + 24$

2) $2x^2 + 4xy + 6y^2$

3) $-2x^3 - 2x^2 + 4x - 1$

4) $x^3y + 3x^2y - 6xy^2 + xy$

5) -22

6) $5x^2 - 5x + 10$

7) $p^4 - 9p^2 - p + 13$

8) $4x^2 + 8$

9) $x^2 + 9x - 10$

10) $-y^5 + 4y^4 + y^2$

Multiplication and Division of Polynomials:

11) $x^2 + 6x + 5$

12) $6x^2 + 8x + 2$

13) $3x^2 - 8x - 3$

14) $x^4 - x^3 + 5x^2 - 9x - 36$

15) $2x^2 + 7x - 30$

16) $6x^4 - 13x^3 - 3x^2 + 29x - 20$

17) $x^2 - \frac{1}{4}x - \frac{1}{8}$

18) $x^4 + 4x^3 - 9.5x^2 - 2x + 4.5$

19) $15a^2 + 12a$

20) $-6x^5 + 4x^4 + 8x^3 - 6x^2$

21) $6x^3y^2z^3 - 3x^2y^2z^4 + 15x^4yz^5$

22) $3x^{11}y^5z^8$

23) $3x^3y^4$

24) $\frac{-24a^2b^2c}{5}$

25) $-3x^3y^5 + 2xy^3$

26) $18a^4b^{-1} - 9a^3b^2$

27) $16x^3 - 9x^2y^2 - 6xy$

28) $18a^2b^2 - 12a^3b + 4a$

29)   3

30) $3pq - q^2 + \frac{2}{q}$

31) $-12x^3 + 120x^2 - 255x + 6022$

32) $-18x^2 + 228x + 2300$

Unit 3 - Exponents

Positive Exponents

1) 81

2) ± 4

3) 5^{20}

4) $\dfrac{x^{12}}{4}$

5) 21^4

6) $32^2 = 1,024$

7) $729x^6y^6$

8) $648a^9$

9) $-a^5b^3$

10) x^{10}

11) $-108x^7y^8$

12) $4^6 = 4,096$

13) $2^{2(2)} = 2^4 = 16$

14) $x = 2$

15) $x = \dfrac{7}{8}$

Negative Exponents

16) $\dfrac{1}{x^9}$

17) $5x^{-4}$

18) $\dfrac{3}{a^2}$

19) $\dfrac{1}{225x^2}$

20) $\dfrac{1024}{x^5}$

21) $\dfrac{y^3}{a^2}$

22) $\dfrac{3}{a^3b^8}$

23) $\dfrac{6}{a^2b^4}$

24) $\dfrac{a^4b}{7}$

25) $\dfrac{3}{a^{15}b^2}$

26) $\dfrac{-24a^8b^2}{5c^3}$

27) $\dfrac{18b^5 - 9a^3}{a^{10} \quad b^2}$

28) $-6ab^5 - 9a^2b^6 + \dfrac{16}{a^5}$

29) $\dfrac{-12a^5}{b^8} + 4a^3 + \dfrac{3b^2}{a^2}$

30) $\dfrac{2}{a^5} - \dfrac{3b^2}{a^2}$

31) $\dfrac{y^5}{3x^7}$

32) $\dfrac{-2x^2}{5y^2}$

33) $10x^{10}y^7$

34) $\dfrac{1}{x^8y}$

Solve for the Variable

35) $x = 3$

36) $a = -3$

37) $a = 6$

38) $b = 180^{1/3}$ $b = 5.65$

Word Problems

39) 3^3

40) $(7xyz)^2$

41) $5 * 10^{-4}$

42) $6.49857 * 10^2$, or

$2.06856\pi * 10^2$

43) $114,048$ in/min

Unit 4 - Radicals and Square Roots

Perfect Squares

a)	1	b)	4	c)	9	d)	16	e)	25
f)	36	g)	49	h)	64	i)	81	j)	100
k)	121	l)	144	m)	169	n)	196	o)	225
p)	256	q)	289	r)	324	s)	361	t)	400
u)	441	v)	484	w)	529	x)	576	y)	625

Practice Problems – Radicals

1) $2\sqrt{10}$

2) $5\sqrt{3}$

3) $3\sqrt[3]{6}$

4) $\pm.11$

5) $\pm.4$

6) $\pm 7y\sqrt{6}$

7) 5

8) -32

9) ± 2

10) $\frac{1}{64}$ or 64^{-1}

11) $\frac{1}{4}$ or 4^{-1}

12) $10,000\sqrt{10}$

13) $3y\sqrt[3]{x}$

14) $2\sqrt[6]{x}$

15) 6

16) $\pm 2\sqrt{5}$

17) $\pm \sqrt{5}$

18) $\pm \frac{4}{5}$

19) $\pm 5\sqrt{3}$

20) $\pm 10\sqrt{2}$

21) ± 6

22) $\frac{4}{3}$

23) $\sqrt{0.5} * \sqrt[4]{8}$

24) $\pm \sqrt{5}$

Practice Problems – Radical Equations

25) $x = 225$

26) $x = 600$

27) $b = 1284$

28) $x = 4$

29) $x = \frac{2}{3}$

30) $(b+8)(b+3), b = -8$ or -3

31) $x = -\frac{1}{6}$

32) $36x^2 + 41x + 12$ (quad. formula)

33) $x^2 + 9x + 29$ (quad. formula)

34) $49x^2 - 61x + 10$ (quad. formula)

Radical Equation Word Problems

35) $\frac{15+\sqrt{321}}{16}$, or ≈ 2.057 seconds

36) $15\sqrt{5}$, or ≈ 33.54 miles

37) 12.2 miles

38) $81 + 41\sqrt{5}$

39) 80 volts

Unit 5 - Factoring

Find the Greatest Common Factor

1) $7x$

2) $4ab$

3) $5ab$

Factor the GCF

4) $2(x^2 - 2)$

5) $4(a - 3)$

6) $4p^2q(q^2 + 6p - 4p^2q)$

7) $-7xz^2(y^2z^2 - 3xy^3 + 12x^2)$

8) $(x + 5)(x - 3)$

9) $(p + 4)(p^2 - 1)$ or
$(p + 4)(p + 1)(p - 1)$

Difference of Two Squares

10) $(x + 6)(x - 6)$

11) $(y + 9)(y - 9)$

12) $(7 + x)(7 - x)$

13) $(x - y - 9)(x - y + 9)$

14) $3(5z - 7b)(5z + 7b)$

15) $(2x - 5)(2x + 11)$

Trinomials

16) $(x - 5)(x - 3)$

17) $(y - 1)(y + 4)$

18) $(x + 4)(x + 8)$

19) $(y + 11)(y + 2)$

20) $(x - 12)(x - 4)$

21) $(y + 6)(y - 3)$

Solving for a variable

22) $x = -1$ or $x = -2$

23) $y = -6$ or $y = 1$

24) $y = -\frac{3}{2}, -1$

25) $x = 0$ or $x = \pm\frac{1}{2}$

26) $y = -16$

27) $x = 3$ or $x = -3$

Sum and Difference of Cubes

28) $(x-4)(x^2 + 2x + 2)$

29) $(x + 4)(x^2 - 4x + 16)$

30) $50(2x - 1)(4x^2 + 2x + 1)$

31) $4(2x - 1)(4x^2 + 2x + 1)$

32) $3(x + 3)(x^2 - 3x + 9)$

33) $5(2x-1)(4x^2 + 2x + 1)$

Grouping

34) $(3x + 4)(10x^2 + 1)$

35) $(x + 2)(9x^2 + 7)$

36) $(3x + 5)(6x^2 + 1)$

37) $(x - 4)(5x^2 + 3)$

38) $(9x - 1)(2x^2 + 3)$

39) $(-1)(x + 2)(2x^2 + 3)$

Evaluate the Discriminant and Number of Solutions

40) 169, 2 real solutions

41) -164, no real solutions

42) -60, no real solutions

43) 2,304, 2 real solutions

44) -112, no real solutions

45) -100, no real solutions

Mastery Unit A

1) $y = \pm\frac{1}{6}$

2) $16\sqrt{6} - 18\sqrt{6} = -2\sqrt{6}$

3) $.16x^6$

4) $\pm\frac{5x}{6}$

5) $x - y = 8$

6) $x - y = 11$

7) $4x - 4y = 8$

8) 12

9) 57

10) $\frac{3x\ +\ 5y}{2} = 12$

11) $x + y = 8$

12) $2(x^2 - y^2) = 16$

13) $y = 7$

14) $x = -3$

15) $\frac{7}{18}$

16) $y = 4$

17) 16 years old

18) 3

19) $x = 315$

20) $c \approx 168.17$

21) $-x^3 - 3x - 50$

22) $960\sqrt{y}$

23) $(ax - 2)(ax + 12) = 0$

24) $x = \frac{-b \pm \sqrt{b^2 - 4ac}}{2a}$

25) One solution: $b^2 - 4ac = 0$

Two solutions: $b^2 - 4ac > 0$

No solutions: $b^2 - 4ac < 0$

Unit 6 – Absolute Value Equations

Absolute Value Equations

1) Solution: $x = \pm 4$,

   Transformation: down 4

   Stretch/Compression: 1, no stretch

   Vertex: (0, -4)

   Line of Symmetry: $x = 0$

2) Solution: $x = -2$ or $x = -4$

   Transformation: down 1, left 3

   Stretch/Compression: 1, no stretch

   Vertex: (-3, -1)

   Line of Symmetry: $x = -3$

3) Algebraic Solution: $x = \frac{2}{3}$ or $x = -\frac{8}{3}$

   Transformation: flips over x axis, up 5, left 1

   Stretch/Compression: stretch factor of 3

   Vertex: (-1, 5)

   Line of Symmetry: $x = -1$

4) Algebraic Solution: $x = 10$ or $x = 2$

   Transformation: down 2, right 6

   Stretch/Comp.: compression, $\frac{1}{2}$

   Vertex: (6, -2)

   Line of Symmetry: $x = 6$

5) Algebraic Solution: $x = 1$ or $x = -5$

   Transformation: down 3, left 2

   Stretch/Compression factor: 1, no stretch

   Vertex: (-2, -3)

   Line of Symmetry: $x = -2$

6) Algebraic Solution: $x = 2$ or $x = 0$

   Trans..: flips over x axis, up 5, right 1

   Stretch/Comp.: stretch factor of 5

   Vertex: (1, 5)

   Line of Symmetry: $x = 1$

Unit 7 – Graphing: Lines, Quadratics, Cubes

Linear Equation Practice Problems

1) Equation: $y = -6x + 32$

   X-intercept: $(\frac{16}{3}, 0)$

   Y-intercept: $(32, 0)$

2) Equation: $y = -x - 5$

   X-intercept: $(-5, 0)$

   Y-intercept: $(0, -5)$

Quadratic Equation Practice Problems

3) Vertex: (-1, -5)

   Axis of Symmetry: $x = -1$

   Min./Max.: Min of -5

   Range: $y \geq -5$, or $[-5, \infty)$

   Domain: $-\infty < x < \infty$, or $(-\infty, \infty)$

4) Vertex: (3, 3)

   Axis of Symmetry: $x = 3$

   Min./Max.: Min of 3

   Range: $y \geq 3$, or $[3, \infty)$

   Domain: $-\infty < x < \infty$, or $(-\infty, \infty)$

Linear and Quadratic Equation Word Problems

5) a. $y = 10x + 175$

   b. 675 pieces

6) $y = 7.50x - 5$

7) $y = 5x + 65$

8) a. $y = 145 - 15x$

   c. 8 days

9) $20

10) ≈ 5.89 seconds

11) ≈ 9.62 seconds

12) 7.8 phones in 2000, 107.8 in 2010

Unit 8 – Linear Systems

Determine if the ordered pair is a solution of the system

1)   no   2)   yes   3)   no   4)   no

Substitution/Linear Combination Problems

5) $x = 8, y = -3$ 6) $x = -\frac{6}{5}, y = \frac{96}{25}$

7) $x = -2, y = 0$ 8) $x = 9, y = -5$

Graphing and stating the solution

9) $x = -2, y = -1$ 10) $x = -1, y = 3$

Matrices

11) $x = 4$
$y = -2$
$z = 6$

12) $x = 1$
$y = 0$
$z = -3$

13) $x = 1$
$y = 2$
$z = -3$

14) $x = -1$
$y = -2$
$z = 2$

Solve the following equations

15)   No Solution   16)   No Solution

17)   No Solution   18) $y - x = -5$

19) $a - b = 4$ 20) $3a - 2b = -14$

Graphing and stating the solutions

21)   a. $c = 10t + 8$

                  $c = 12t$

     b. $c = 48, \ t = 4$; this point represents the number of tickets you would need to buy for the cost of ordering tickets online to equal the cost of buying them at the door.

22)   27 right-handed, 3 left-handed

23)   no solution, they never intersect   24)   intersects at $x = .69$ and $x = 22.04$

25) $t \approx 7.81$ seconds

Unit 9 – Inequalities

1) $x \geq -\dfrac{1}{3}$

2) $x \geq -23$

3) $x > \dfrac{13}{7}$

4) $-\dfrac{5}{6} < x < -\dfrac{1}{3}$

5) $8 \leq x \leq 88$

6) $-2 < x < 5$

7) $a > c$

8) $x < 5$

9) $x < 12$

10) $l > b > j$

Absolute Value Inequalities

11) $x \leq -7, \qquad x \geq 27$

12) $x \leq \dfrac{3}{22}, \qquad x \geq -\dfrac{15}{22}$

13) $x \leq 13, \qquad x \geq -14$

14) $x \leq -56, \qquad x \geq -16$

15) $p \leq \dfrac{8}{3}, \qquad p \geq 0$

16) $x \leq \dfrac{-35}{3}, \qquad x \geq 5$

17) $89.95 \leq l \leq 90.05$

18) $28.5 \leq c \leq 29$

19) maximum height = 5 ft. 3 in.

    minimum height = 4 ft. 9 in.

Unit 10 – Fractions

Adding and Subtracting Like and Unlike Fractions

1) $\frac{1}{2}$

2) $\frac{2}{3}$

3) $5\frac{1}{2}$

4) $\frac{8}{9}$

5) $\frac{3}{8}$

6) $\frac{8}{9}$

7) $\frac{27}{8}$ or $3\frac{3}{8}$

8) 4

9) $11\frac{23}{27}$

10) 3

11) $\frac{(x+3)(x-1)}{5(x+4)}$

12) $\frac{2x-1}{4x^2}$

13) $\frac{4}{x^4}$

14) $\frac{7x^2}{x+49}$

15) $\frac{4x^2}{(x+1)^2}$

16) $\frac{(x+1)(x-7)(x-5)}{9(x+5)}$

17) $\frac{28}{39}$

18) $\frac{9}{7}$

19) $7\frac{1}{21}$

20) $\frac{16}{63}$

Solve twice

21) $x^2 - 2x + 4 - \frac{7}{3x+1}$

22) $6x^4 + 6x^3 + 10x^2 + 10x + 9 + \frac{9}{x+1}$

23) $x^3 + 7x + 5$

24) $x^2 + 6x + 9$

Practice Problems

25) $\frac{x}{z} = \frac{2}{5}$

26) $x = 3$

27) $x = -3$ or $x = -4$

28) $x^2 - 25x - 36 = 0$ (quad. form.)

29) $\frac{7}{9}$

30) $e = \frac{a}{d+1}$

31) $-v$

Mastery Unit B

1) $\dfrac{2ed}{e-d}$

2) $\dfrac{1}{6}$

3) $5x^3 - 22x^2 - 3x - 53$

4) $(x+1)$ by $(x+2)$ by $(x+3)$

5) $x = 2,\ y = -1$

6) After buying 24 CDs

7) When he has used 15.18 GB of data

8) $(.725, 4.175)$, $(8.27, 26.82)$

9) 0 times

10) $y > \dfrac{1}{3}x - 2$

11) $\$29,166.67$

12) Equation: $y = -6x - 37$

   X-intercept: $(-6\frac{1}{6}, 0)$

   Y- intercept: $(0, -37)$

13) Equation: $y = x$

   X-intercept: $(0, 0)$

   Y-intercept: $(0, 0)$

14) Equation: $y = -2|x+3| + 3$

   Transformation: flipped, up 3 left 3

   Stretch/Comp.: stretch factor of 2

   Vertex: $(-3, 3)$

   Line of Symmetry: $x = -3$

15) Equation: $y \geq |x+8| - 8$

   Transformation: left 8, down 8

   Stretch/Compression: none

   Vertex: $(-8, -8)$

   Line of Symmetry: $x = -8$

Unit 11 – Proportions, Ratios, Percentages, Growth & Decay

Set in a ration/fraction and simplify

1) $\dfrac{1}{11}$

2) $\dfrac{2}{3}$

3) $\dfrac{13}{40}$

4) $\dfrac{1}{3}$

Set as a unit rate

5) 39.6 mpg

6) $14.00 per ticket

7) 4.5 inches of snow per hour

8) $670.00 per person

Solve for the variable

9) $m = 21$

10) $x = 1$

11) $r = 1.6$

12) $x = 2.1$

Express each fraction as a percent

13) 31 %

14) 37.5 %

15) 66.7 %

16) 120 %

Solve

17) 24

18) 24

19) 6

20) 22

21) 40 %

22) 12.5 %

23) 6.25 %

24) 0.5 %

25) 140

26) 25 %

27) 40

28) 60

Word problems

29) a) $2317.85

b) $2416.08

c) $2439.28

d) $2450.69

e) $2451.08

30) a) $2,193,162.97

b) $2,363,169.45

c) $2,404,446.58

d) $2,424,902.26

e) $2,425,608.68

31) $16,704.20

32) 20 hours

33) a) $112,362.00

b) $95,310.06

c) $80,845.90

34) $65.80

35) $3,600

Unit 12– Basic Statistics

Define:

Mean/Average: The sum of the data divided by the number of individual data units.

Mode: The item that occurs most frequently in a data set.

Median: The middle number or the average of the two middle numbers when the data set is listed in order from least to greatest.

Scatter Plot: A graph that shows the relationship between two sets of data.

1) Mean: 157.80
    Mode: None
    Median: 155

2) Mean: 45.86
    Mode: 25
    Median: 36

3) Mean: 1.09
    Mode: None
    Median: $\frac{3}{4}$

4) $x = 5.5$

5) Average: $x - 1$

6) $y = \frac{4}{3}$

7) 22

8) 86

9) 91

10) 15

11) Mode: 8
     Median: 8

12) $x + y = 10$

13) 9

Unit 13 – Functions

1) Domain: $\{-2, -1, 0, 1, 2\}$

2) yes, x values do not repeat

3) Domain: $\{3, 4, 7\}$
   Range: $\{-1, 0, 1\}$

4) no, x values repeat

5) $f(-1) = -8$

6) $f(10) = -137$

7) $h(x) = 3x - 5$

8) $h(x) = x - 3$

9) $h(x) = -x - 1$

10) $h(x) = 3x - 4$

11) $h(x) = 2x^2 - 6x + 4$

12) $h(x) = \frac{2x - 4}{x - 1}$

13) $h(x) = 2x - 6$

14) $h(x) = 2x - 5$

15) $f(x)^{-1} = \frac{x - 22}{11}$

16) $f(x)^{-1} = 2x + 10$

17) $f(x)^{-1} = \pm\sqrt{x + 1}$

Unit 14 - Imaginary Numbers

1) i

2) $\pm 6i$

3) $\pm 12i\sqrt{x}$

4) $i\sqrt{254}$

5) $a - bi$

6) $a + bi$

7) $5 + 6i$

8) $5 - 6i$

9) $11 + 3i$

10) $30 - 5i$

11) $-2 + 7i$

12) $-25 + 52i$

13) $i\sqrt{35}$

14) $9i$

15) $-i$

16) $-35i$

17) 7

18) $3i$

19) -12

20) 6

21) $\dfrac{-12i\sqrt{7}}{7}$

22) $\dfrac{i}{4}$

23) $-24i$

24) -15

25) $\dfrac{30+5i}{37}$

26) $x^2 + 3x - 2ix - 6i$

27) $x - 3i$

28) $\dfrac{x+6i}{x^2+36}$

29) $\dfrac{7-26i}{25}$

30) $39 - 80i$

31) $x = \pm i$

32) $7 + 11i$

33) $-24i - 60$

34) $-1 \pm 3i$

35) $\dfrac{5 \pm i\sqrt{11}}{-6}$

Unit 15 – Basic Trigonometry

1) a. $\frac{1}{2}$ d. $\frac{\sqrt{3}}{2}$

    b. $\frac{\sqrt{3}}{2}$ e. $\frac{1}{2}$

    c. $\frac{\sqrt{3}}{3}$ f. $\sqrt{3}$

2) a. $\frac{\sqrt{2}}{2}$

    b. $\frac{\sqrt{2}}{2}$

    c. 1

3) a. $\frac{4}{5}$ d. $\frac{3}{5}$

    b. $\frac{3}{5}$ e. $\frac{4}{5}$

    c. $\frac{4}{3}$ f. $\frac{3}{4}$

4) Cos: $\frac{\sqrt{3}}{2}$

    Tan: $\frac{\sqrt{3}}{3}$

5) Cos: $\frac{2\sqrt{2}}{3}$

    Tan: $\frac{\sqrt{2}}{4}$

6) Cos: $\frac{8}{17}$

    Tan: $\frac{8}{15}$

7) Sin: $\frac{12}{13}$

    Tan: $\frac{12}{5}$

8) Cos: $\frac{5\sqrt{26}}{26}$

    Sin: $\frac{\sqrt{26}}{26}$

9) Cos: $\frac{4}{5}$

    Sin: $\frac{3}{5}$

Mastery Unit C

1) $x = 2z - 6$

2) 89.2

3) 91.67%

4) 80%

5) 80 men

6) 2400 eggs

7) 20 pairs of jeans

8) $f^{-1}(x) = -\frac{3}{2}x + \frac{3}{2}$

9) $i^7 = -i$

10) a. $337,209.30

b. $453,125.00

c. $690,476.19

11) 36 hours

12) $\cos\theta = \frac{4}{5}, \tan\theta = \frac{3}{4}$

13) 184.9 miles

14) a. $(f * g)(x) = 2x^3 - 5x^2 + 5x + 4$

b. $(f + g)(x) = x^2 - x + 5$

c. $(f - g)(x) = -x^2 + 5x - 3$

15) $\sin F = \frac{5}{13}$

16) 928,800 flakes

17) $\frac{12-5i}{26}$

18) $\tan K = \frac{\sqrt{21}}{2}$

19) a. 160 fries

b. 5 minutes

20) $f(g(x)) = -2x^2 + 14$

$g(f(x)) = -4x^2 - 16x - 11$

21) $\frac{i}{2}$

22) $\sin\theta = \frac{\sqrt{2}}{2}$

23) $f(2) = 22, f(-5) = 92$

24) $28.50

25) $\sin(90° - x°) = \frac{3}{5}$

26) -25

27) $x = 1$

28) sides $= 10$, hypotenuse $= 10\sqrt{2}$

29) $f^{-1}(7) = 2$

30) d) $12\sin 25°$

31) a. $12,762.82

b. $12,820.37

c. $12,840.25

32) $AB = 20, \; AC = 10\sqrt{3}$

33) $48 + 6i$

34) 248,623,402

35) $a = 5$

36) $45.79 each

Geometry Answers

Unit 1 - Angles

1)   1 = 138°   5 = 138°
           2 = 42°   6 = 42°
           3 = 42°   7 = 42°
           4 = 138°   8 = 138°

2)   1 = $y°$
           2 = $(180 - y)°$
           3 = $(180 - y)°$
           4 = $y°$

3)   1 = 110°   5 = 110°
           2 = 70°   6 = 70°
           3 = 70°   7 = 70°
           4 = 110°   8 = 110°

4)   a = 140°   e = 155°
           b = 40°   f = 25°
           c = 40°   g = 25°
           d = 140°   h = 155°

5) $\angle FOE = 45°$ $\angle AOH = 45°$
           $\angle EOD = 45°$ $\angle HOG = 54°$
           $\angle DOC = 54°$ $\angle GOE = 81°$
           $\angle COB = 36°$ $\angle BOH = 90°$
           $\angle BOA = 45°$

6) $x = 35°$, larger angle $= 120°$

7) $x = 18°$, larger angle $= 120°$

8) $\angle ABC = 76°$

9)   Sum of the angles $= 90°$

10) $\angle BOA = 122°$

Unit 2 - Triangles

1) $x = 55°$, acute, scalene

2) $x = 91°$, obtuse, scalene

3) $x = 60°$, equilateral, equiangular
       $y = 6$,
       $z = 6$

4) $x = 45°$, scalene, acute

5) $x = 20°$, scalene, obtuse

6) $x = 95°$, scalene, obtuse

7) $a = 40°$ $z = 100°$
       $b = 140°$
       $x = 140°$
       $y = 40°$

8) $a = 108°$ $e = 37°$
       $b = 44°$ $f = 145°$
       $c = 145°$ $g = 11°$
       $d = 35°$

9) $a = 15°$ $e = 40°$ $i = 83°$
       $b = 100°$ $f = 83°$ $j = 70°$
       $c = 80°$ $g = 123°$ $k = 70°$
       $d = 65°$ $h = 57°$

10) $x = 24$

11) $y = 8$

12)   Both triangles are equiangular/equilateral by side-angle-side. The triangles are similar.

13)   The triangles are right, congruent. They may be proved congruent by ASA or SAS. Congruent.

14) $t = 11°$

15) $\angle ABC = 79°$

16)   Area $= 16\sqrt{3}$ units^2

17) $2.25\sqrt{3}$ feet^2

18) $x = 4$ inches

19)   Area $= 64\sqrt{3}$ units^2

20) $y/2 = 3$

21) $a = 5$
$b = 5$

22) $x = 5$
$y = 5\sqrt{3}$
$a = 60°$

23) $a = 60°$
$b = 30°$
$x = 18$

24) $x = 3$
$y = 3\sqrt{2}$
$a = 45°$
$b = 45°$

25) $x = 7\sqrt{2}$
$y = 7\sqrt{2}$
$a = 45°$
$b = 45°$
Area $= 16$ units^2

26) $32\sqrt{3} + 192$ inches^2

27) $x + y = 145°$

28) Ratio $= 5/12$

29) $x^2 + y^2 = 200$

30) Ratio $= 25/1$

31) $RS = 6$

32) $a = 80°$ $e = 50°$
$b = 50°$ $f = 60°$
$c = 130°$ $g = 70°$
$d = 120°$

Unit 3 - Polynomials with 360° or Greater

1) $a = 180°$ $f = 900°$
   $b = 360°$ $g = 1080°$
   $c = 360°$ $h = 1260°$
   $d = 540°$ $l = 1440°$
   $e = 720°$

2) Fourth angle $= 150°$

3) $x = 73°$ but the smallest angle $= 78°$

4) $142°, 38°, 142°$

5) Diagonals $= 24\sqrt{2}$ feet; Perimeter $= 96$ feet; Area $= 576$ feet^2

6) $a = 3$
   $b = 8$

7) 6 triangles

8) $22.51\sqrt{3}$ units^2

9) $120°$

10) $x = 60°$

11) Perimeter $= 36$ units; Area $= 52$ units^2

12) 4

13) $AC = 3\sqrt{2}$
    $DE = \frac{3\sqrt{2}}{2}$

14) $\angle NQM = 110°$
    $\angle MRO = 180°$
    $\angle ORP = 110°$
    $\angle NPO = 35°$

15) $BC = 18.14$

Unit 4 - Circles

1) a. BE, CG, DF   e. 10
    b. BE, DF   f. 8π
    c. AB, AE, DA, AF   g. 36π
    d. CG

2) $a = 5\sqrt{2} * \pi$ inches
    $b = 12.5\pi$ inches^2

3) a) 9π
    b) $36 - 9\pi$ feet^2 or 7.7 feet^2

4) a) Area $= 72.25\pi$ yards^2
    b) Circumference $= 17\pi$ yards
    c) Area not in the rectangle $= (72.25\,\pi - 120$ yards$^2)$ or 107 yards^2

5) Area of circle $= 16\pi$ feet^2
    Area of $\Delta = 16$ feet^2
    Perimeter of $\Delta = 8\sqrt{2} + 8$ feet
    Area not in the $\Delta = 64\pi - 16$ feet^2

6) a) $\angle CAD = 30°$
    b) $\angle DAE = 90°$
    c) $\angle FAE = 60°$
    d) $\angle FAB = 30°$
    e) $\angle BAC = 150°$
    f) $\angle CAF = 180°$

7) a) $CD = \pi$ cm
    b) $DE = 3\pi$ cm
    c) $FB = \pi$ cm
    b) $BE = 3\pi$ cm
    e) $FC = 6\pi$ cm

8) a) $CAD = 4.1\pi$ cm^2
    b) $DAF = 20.4\pi$ cm^2
    c) $FAB = 4.1\pi$ cm^2

9) $x = 30°$
    Smallest angle $= 25°$
    Largest angle $= 90°$

10) Circumference is multiplied by 3, the area is multiplied by 9 (square of the ratios of circumference/ratio)

11) Area of the sector $= 6\pi$ inches^2

12) $2\frac{5}{8}$ inches^2

13) 225π or 706.86 feet^2

14) 13.5π inches^3

16) 10,560 feet
1345 revolutions

17) $x = 33°$
Smallest angle $= 38°$
Largest angle $= 99°$

18) Diameter $= 9$

19) Area $= 32\pi - 16$ feet^2

20) $1 : 4$

Mrs. Ross' Baker's Dozen of Reminders

- *Trust no one*: Beware of the college marketing machine who promises to get you into ANY school. Beware of the SAT program that will increase your scores hundreds of points with no effort on your part. Beware of anyone who tells you that the College Admissions process is really, really simple or really, really hard. It does not have to be either – just systematic.

- *Guard your privacy*: If you are a junior or senior, you know that people will ask you the most outlandish questions about your grades, SAT's, extracurricular activities, etc. Decide early on how much you want to share. Make an agreement with your parents and stick to it. Develop a pat answer to the nosy questions and USE it!

- *Stay out of the fray*: Don't get caught up in the competition. You are not working toward a prize; you are working toward an education that will fit you academically, athletically, socially and financially. Your prize is not anyone else's.

- *Look through the camera lens*: As you move through the College Admissions Process, imagine that you are carrying a camera. Look out through that viewfinder and judge what the colleges have to offer you. And then on every step of the journey from developing your résumé to visiting the colleges to interviewing to writing your essays and requesting your letters of recommendation, imagine yourself as the college Admissions Officer looking out that same camera and finding you in the viewfinder. What DO you have to offer and how are you going to communicate it? How do those bored, texting students on the campus visits look to you now?

- *Don't buy the urban legends*: Students and parents tell me all the time, "oh we can't consider that school; it's a party school." When I ask them how they know, they never have a real answer. One of Virginia colleges has the reputation of having a high suicide rate. Recently one of my students decided not to attend the school because of this urban legend. When I offered to research the topic to help her make her decision, she turned me and one of the best schools in the country down, based on high school rumors.

- *No whining*: I cannot emphasize this dictum enough. Many students have to explain low grades or difficult times. Still, make sure that you grow and learn from your adversity and that you communicate the growth and not the difficulty.

- *Neatness counts*: Another important one – errors can break your college application. Remember Daniela's application essay to William and Mary in which she stated that she looked forward to four years at the University of DELAWARE!

- *Check your arrogance*: Whether it is a defensive move or just sheer inexperience, some students give off an unfortunate air of arrogance. Nothing and I mean nothing, turns off goodwill like arrogance. Remember that all of the adults with whom you are interacting have already been 16, 17 and 18 years old. Treat everyone with respect AND kindness. Some of the processes to apply to college, order your transcripts, or register for the SAT may seem stupid but there is no way around them.

- *Ask and you shall receive*: College Admissions Officers are there to work with you. Before requesting help, though, make sure to do your research. Knowledge is very powerful in this process. If something is not clear to you, ask. If you need additional help with financial aid, research and then ask.

- *Keep in touch*: College Admissions Officers try really hard but most cannot read minds. Remember to help develop cohesion in your application package by keeping in touch with your Admissions Officer.

- *Be true to yourself*: Students often ask me if they should exclude religious or political organizations from their résumés. They worry that the colleges will take exception to their views. Colleges are looking for well-rounded students with lots of interests. So, if you are in the Young Republicans or Young Democrats or Future Business Leaders of America, stand and be proud or your involvement. If you belong to the Fellowship of Christian Athletes, a church youth group, Hillel or any other religious group, include these activities on your résumé IF you participate and IF they are important to you. Honestly, if any college or university would look down on a student for having political views or religious affiliations, you should take your application and run in the opposite direction!

- *Keep your eye on the ball*: The ball is a first-rate education that will prepare you for the world. Remember that your goal is to shine and to find the right colleges for you, not the right college for your parents or grandparents or neighbors or anyone else. If it does not feel right, remember the Designer Shoe Syndrome and step back. It is you who will live and study and sleep on this college campus for four years.

- *Keep your chin up*: There are almost 4000 colleges in the United States. Many accept 80%, 90% or even 100% of applicants. There is a college for you, many colleges for you!

Again, I hope that you have enjoyed our journey together. I would love to hear from you. Visit me at JuliaRossPT.com. Godspeed...

GETTING INTO COLLEGE

with

Julia Ross

FINDING THE RIGHT FIT
AND MAKING IT HAPPEN

Julia Ross

Principal, Professional Tutoring, LLC

SECOND EDITION

Preview of

Getting into College

with Julia Ross

Finding the Right Fit and Making It Happen, 2nd Edition

Foreword

Here I sit, in tears, completely panicked. Not only am I facing my senior year of high school but I have the daunting task of looking for a college that is the right fit for me (not my parents). I have to fit in class work, essays for college admissions, and applications for college while enjoying my senior year. My parents are driving me crazy because all they talk about is college. Sometimes a little outside guidance is necessary, and this book is just that.

Finding the right fit can be difficult, but not impossible. Do not misunderstand, no college is perfect; however, the likelihood of searching for and finding the right college is possible. The teenage years are frustrating, caught between childhood and adulthood; the simplest tasks can seem impossible. Of course, asking parents for help is something I really do not want to do; at least, I'd never admit to wanting parental help. With everything that needs to be completed before even applying to colleges including tours, interviews, and résumés, stress can build up and become unbearable. The largest problem that occurs when searching for a college is maintaining your identity and reassuring yourself that all will work out.

Organizing what I need is one of the hurdles that I have to overcome in the next few months. Figuring out what type of college environment I want to be in is the next step in the process. Although you may have encountered friends or family members that will share their triumphant and horrific college search stories, remember, yours will be different. However, the only way to ensure the difference is this book. This book will be guiding light needed by you and your parents to remain sane through this insane process of finding the "right" colleges and getting in. Never mind paying for four years of advanced education.

Finding the right fit is needed to ensure success, but most importantly happiness. If you are unhappy, it is hard to be successful. Trust me, I know from experience; sophomore chemistry was a killer. College is the next step toward your future, not your parents' future, your future. I need to emphasize the fact that this is your decision, because I know that all parents want the best for us, even though they may appear overbearing at times. I am also in the middle of this overwhelming process. Still I always feel relieved after reading even a chapter of this book. This book will allow you to escape the overwhelming feelings that may envelope you at times. This book will allow you to discover where you want to be and what you want to do in life. The majority of students looking at colleges have no idea what they want to major in or what they want in life. But, that is perfectly normal. Discover where you want to be with the help of this book, and the rest will come in time. Looking for the right school is important, but with the right outlook, it can also be fun. So, de-stress and enjoy the moments ahead, because this is only the beginning.

—*Samantha Mullen, at the beginning of senior year*

Chapter 1: The College Selection Journey

In this chapter:

- Meet Colin, Grace, and Ally, three ordinary students. Follow their extraordinary success.

- Timelines designed to guide you through your own successful college selection journey.

Chapter 2: Developing Your Personal College List

In this chapter:

- Work through 18 decision criteria to target your college matches.

- Compile a list of colleges that suit you.

- Sneak a peek at Colin, Grace, and Ally's Selection Spreadsheets so that you can develop your own.

Chapter 3: The Numbers Game

In this chapter:

- Learn the ins and outs of the SATs and ACTs.

- Get great test day advice!

- Rate your potential colleges: Safety, Attainable, and Reach.

- Learn what not to do in Silly Student Stories!

Chapter 4: Developing Your Student Resume

In this chapter:

- Explore the Student Résumé, cornerstone of The College Coaching Program.

- Read Colin, Grace, and Ally's résumés with Julia's commentary.

- Fill out the worksheets to start your own résumé.

Chapter 5: Tackling College Applications

In this chapter:

- Early Decision, Early Action, Rolling Admissions, the Common Application... learn which will work for you.

- Make an application plan and follow it through to success.

- Learn how to avoid common application pitfalls.

Chapter 6: Letters of Recommendation

In this chapter:

- Learn how to choose your recommenders and to effectively request strong letters of recommendation.

- Read Colin and Grace's requests and letters of recommendation.

- Develop your own ideas.

Chapter 7: Application Essays

In this chapter:

- Learn why some essays are successful and why others bomb!

- Follow our three students through their essays and Julia's intuitive critiques.

- Read the hilarious "Questionable Judgment" Essays.

Chapter 8: Giving and Receiving an Impression

In this chapter:

- Learn how to make the most of your college visits and how to open doors other students don't even know exist!

- "Romance the Admissions Officer."

Chapter 9: Specialized Applications

In this chapter:

- Learn the requirements for ROTC programs and how to apply to the five U.S. Service Academies.

- Read a winning letter of recommendation to the U.S. Naval Academy.

- Learn how to write an Athletic or Music résumé.

Chapter 10: Show Me the Money: Scholarships and Financial Aid

In this chapter:

- Did you know that the vast majority of merit scholarships are awarded by individual colleges?

- Learn how to position yourself to receive thousands of dollars in merit awards, not loans, not grants, and not work study.

Chapter 11: Fare Thee Well

Made in the USA
Middletown, DE
26 February 2023

25443545R00170